MARGARET BOYLES' COUNTRY NEEDLEWORK

MARGARET BOYLES' COUNTRY NEEDLEWORK

MARGARET BOYLES

HARPER & ROW, PUBLISHERS, New York
Cambridge, Philadelphia, San Francisco, London
Mexico City, São Paulo, Singapore, Sydney

1817

BOMC offers recordings and compact discs, cassettes and records. For information and catalog write to BOMR, Camp Hill, PA 17012.

Designer: Ulrich Ruchti

Library of Congress Cataloging-in-Publication Data

Boyles, Margaret.
    Margaret Boyles' country needlework.

    Includes index.
    1. Needlework. I. Title. II. Title: Country needle-
work.
TT750.B7   1986   746.4   86-2314
ISBN 0-06-181099-1

CONTENTS

A section of color photographs follows page 64.

INTRODUCTION

There's something magic about a country interior, something elusive that tugs at our heartstrings, something compelling in a collection of folk art and handcrafted furniture that recalls for us and creates in us a longing for a simpler way of life rooted in the traditions and values we cherish.

Riding this wave of nostalgia, the country decorating theme has awakened an interest in all manner of solid, homely antiques and collectibles long ignored by all but a few inveterate collectors. Suddenly we have all found new appreciation of the skills and artistry of country craftsmen and resurrected the handsome old pieces that had been stored as if awaiting this renaissance. These ties to the past, loved and mellowed with age, are now the centerpieces of wonderful, relaxing country homes. Most of these antiques are still sturdy, usable, and unassumingly beautiful.

Although it is rooted in tradition and composed of the familiar and homespun things we grew up with, this country style of decorating is very difficult to describe. We all recognize it when we see it, but its variations are almost endless. It can be as spare and artistically perfect as a Shaker meeting house or so abundant—filled with baskets, textiles, and collections—that the line between comfort and clutter becomes very fine. It is a look that can be achieved in a city apartment, an eighteenth-century farmhouse, a '50s tract house, or a modern condominium. It is an atmosphere that brings comfort, an indefinable peace, and a sense of history to the places where it is used.

Basically it seems to be a state of mind translated into home furnishings. It consists of our own personal possessions combined with just the right country accents to create a mellow atmosphere that showcases the things that mean the most to us. One wonderful piece of furniture or a collection of antique toys, tools, baskets, or quilts can be the key to the country look.

Needlework, especially old needlework, is a very important part of the country feeling. Samplers, quilts, coverlets, canvas pieces, and primitive hooked rugs add graceful notes of beauty and fragile reminders of the past. Old finds are collected, treasured, displayed, and used with pride.

Good old examples of any of the country arts are becoming scarce and expensive. So building a collection requires care and patience. New needlework can add to a growing accumulation of treasures if it is designed with references to old techniques and designs.

Those of us who have a reverence for old textiles and needle art know there is no way a newly hooked rug, even with a properly naive primitive design, can ever replace the wonderful patina and magic of an antique discovered in the back room of a country shop. But most of us also recognize that the romance of those finds is not always available to all—and in addition there is a real need for some new things that will fit with our growing collection but can be used without worry. That old rug should hang on the wall to preserve its fragile backing, but the new one can be put on the floor in front of the kitchen sink!

The pieces in this book recall old

textiles in a way that makes them adaptable to today's country interiors. They may be mixed with family heirlooms, or they may be used by themselves to add a touch of whimsy to any room. Making new pieces perpetuates the traditions established by women of the past who sought beauty wherever they could find it and gave us the folk art we so cherish. The country style is firmly established as an American classic. Perhaps some of the things we make today will be our contribution to the future. I hope you will enjoy putting together some of your own collectibles from the designs in this book.

To help you do this, I've designed a collection of country accents using many of our favorite needlework techniques, including quilting, patchwork, counted cross stitch, Bargello, needlepoint, and rug hooking. These projects have been grouped together by technique, but the naive designs were planned to be worked in any number of the stitching methods. To illustrate this possibility, several actually have been used for more than one project. Hopefully, these illustrations will inspire you to use the designs to create your own.

Each project is shown both in color and in black and white. With each project is a list of materials, working instructions, and all charts and drawings that are needed. When a particular technique, stitch, or construction is first mentioned it appears in boldface type, indicating that instructions for it exist in **The Basics** section at the back of the book. Here, you will find directions for every technique used, plus individual stitch and construction instructions. This organization makes duplication of the photographed projects an easy task

and helps you make changes if you wish.

You may have antiques you have often thought about copying or adapting to new uses but thought the task too difficult. The methods used to make my accessories should motivate you to begin. Go ahead, copy the border motif from that wonderful old hooked rug and stencil it on a pillow to quilt. That small undertaking may be successful enough to encourage you to stencil the entire border on the walls!

You may have dreamed about making a patchwork quilt, may even have a box of remnants that you have been collecting for that quilt but just never got around to it. Begin by making one of the patchwork pillows; you'll find the piecing intriguing, relaxing, and less time consuming than you thought. The finished pillow, ruffled and plump, will make you want to start that quilt—now you know that quilts grow one square at a time and that there is pleasure and peace in each colorful square.

Like the patchwork pillows, most of my country accessories are easy to make but, as in true folk art tradition, radiate the joy of everyday objects produced by our own hands. Whether you are adding to a growing collection of antiques or using the designs to establish a country atmosphere in your home, I hope you will use the many ideas in the book not only as they are shown but also as a bridge toward making your own versions of the treasured pieces of the past we all revere and cherish. My best wishes for many happy hours!

Margaret Boyles

8

THE DESIGNS

COUNTRY DOLLS

The most important ingredient in the American folk doll is love. Whether made from carefully hoarded scraps of fabric, or nuts, apples, corn husks, clothespins, or wood, each is unique and constructed with loving care. Old ones are collected and displayed along with the finest antiques and truly add a touch of whimsy to a room that is designed around the country theme.

The women who made the old dolls didn't have our precise sewing patterns and wide choice of materials. They began with whatever materials were on hand and made the best doll possible from those. Most were basically simple and sweet, and since each doll maker worked in her own way, it is hard to find two that are exactly alike.

These dolls have the old look and easy construction found in some of the collectible dolls. You'll find it fun to re-create them and fill a basket or shelf with dolls.

Size: 17″ and 13″ high

MATERIALS

For either size doll:
muslin—¼ yard
black cotton fabric—12″ x 16″
print fabric for dress—⅜ yard
black crewel yarn—1 yard
handkerchief or white cotton for
    apron—10″ to 12″ square
fiberfill—a one-pound bag will stuff
    both dolls
⅛″-wide elastic—6″
¼″-wide elastic—10″
snaps—2 small
embroidery floss: blue, black, pink—
    very small quantities of each
cotton lace, 1″ wide—½ yard
transfer pencil
heavy tracing paper
blue washout pen
crewel needle

INSTRUCTIONS

NOTE: All seam allowances for dolls and clothing are ¼″ unless otherwise noted. Antique the fabrics for the doll and clothing before cutting (see **Antiquing Fabrics**). Trace the pattern pieces onto the paper and cut them out on the lines, noting that seam allowances are included on the clothing pieces but not on the doll pattern. With a transfer pencil, trace the doll face on a small piece of paper.

Doll

Lay the body-head pattern piece on the muslin, close to one edge. Use a blue washout pen to trace around the outline (the ink bleeds through so the out-

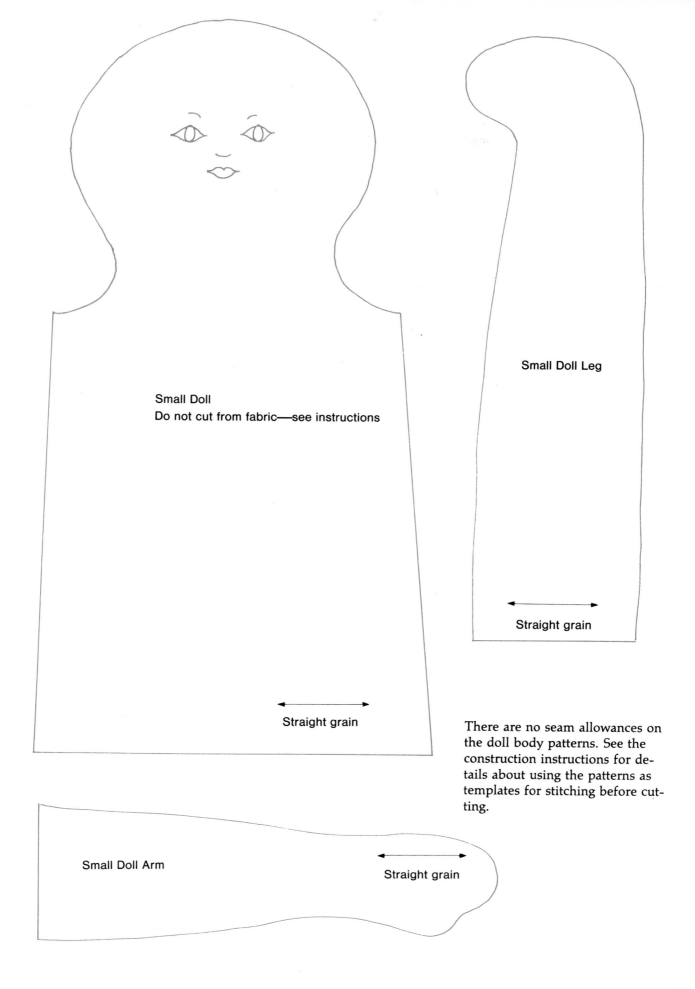

Small Doll
Do not cut from fabric—see instructions

Straight grain

Small Doll Leg

Straight grain

Small Doll Arm

Straight grain

There are no seam allowances on the doll body patterns. See the construction instructions for details about using the patterns as templates for stitching before cutting.

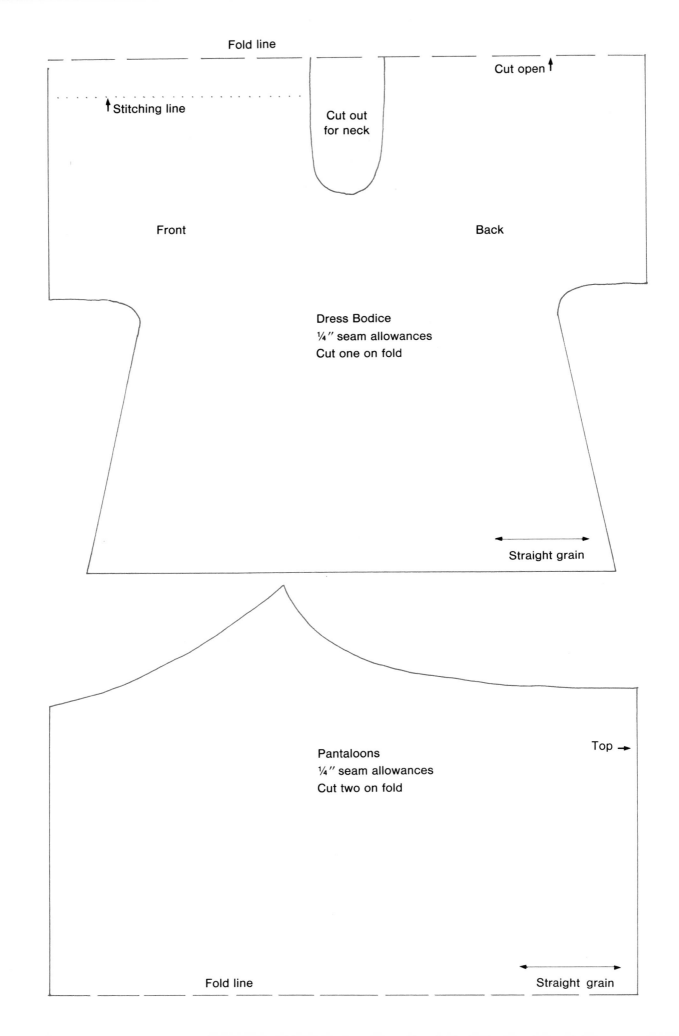

Fold line

Stitching line

Cut out
for neck

Cut open

Front

Back

Dress Bodice
¼″ seam allowances
Cut one on fold

Straight grain

Pantaloons
¼″ seam allowances
Cut two on fold

Top

Fold line

Straight grain

line is visible on both sides of the fabric).

Transfer the face pattern to the muslin, placing it as in the drawing. Embroider the features, using a single strand of embroidery floss throughout. Use blue **satin stitch** for the pupils, pink satin stitch for the mouth. Use tiny black **back stitches** for the eyebrows, nose, and outline of the eyes.

With the right side inside, fold the muslin over and pin the two layers together along the outline of the body-head. Leaving the bottom open, stitch the front to the back on the blue outline. Cut out the stitched piece, leaving ¼″ seam allowances. Clip at the neck curve. Turn right side out. If traces of transfer pencil and washout pen are visible, wash to remove them. Iron to dry fabric. Stuff the head firmly with fiberfill. Leave the body to be stuffed later.

Fold the black fabric in half. Pin the leg pattern to the fabric, placing it so there will be room for the other leg and ¼″ seam allowance all around each. Stitch around the pattern piece, using it as a template and leaving the top of the leg open. Repeat for the other leg. Cut out the two, allowing ¼″ seam allowances and clipping at the ankle curves. Turn right side out and stuff firmly.

Make the arms from muslin, using the pattern pieces as templates and leaving the tops open. Cut, trim, and stuff as you did with the legs. Turn the raw edges at the top to the inside and whip-stitch them together. Stitch the arms to the upper body, taking care to sew them so the thumbs are facing forward.

Lay the body-head section face up on a flat surface. Pin the legs to the right side of the front of the body, raw edges together and toes pointing

downward. Stitch in place. Finish stuffing the body. Turn the raw edges of the body to the inside and whip-stitch to close the opening.

With a large crewel needle and two strands of black crewel yarn, make a row of **French knots** on the seam line of the head, placing the knots about ¼″ apart.

At this point extra **antiquing** can be added to the doll body. Make about ½ cup of strong coffee mixture and add ½ teaspoon of vinegar. Slightly dampen the doll by rubbing water on it with your hand so the coffee will bleed into the fabric rather than leaving harsh or sharp lines. Paint the solution on. I add dye along the seam lines of hands, arms, and head, making the dyed area fairly wide on the head. Putting the doll right into the clothes dryer makes the solution concentrate in a mottled way I like.

Clothing
Pantaloons Cut these from a double layer of muslin, placing the long straight edge on the fold of the fabric as noted on the pattern piece. Open the pieces flat and stitch them together along the front and back crotch seams.

Hem the legs and attach the lace. Match the front seam to the back seam, right sides together, and stitch the legs beginning at the lower inside edge of one and ending at the bottom of the other. Make a ½″ casing at the waist and insert the 10″ piece of elastic.
Dress For the large doll cut out a rectangular skirt piece 9½″ x 28″. For the small doll make the piece 7″ x 22″. Measure 3″ down from the short edge and make a narrow rolled hem to this mark on each short side. With right sides together, sew the hemmed sides together in a ¼″ seam beginning ¼″

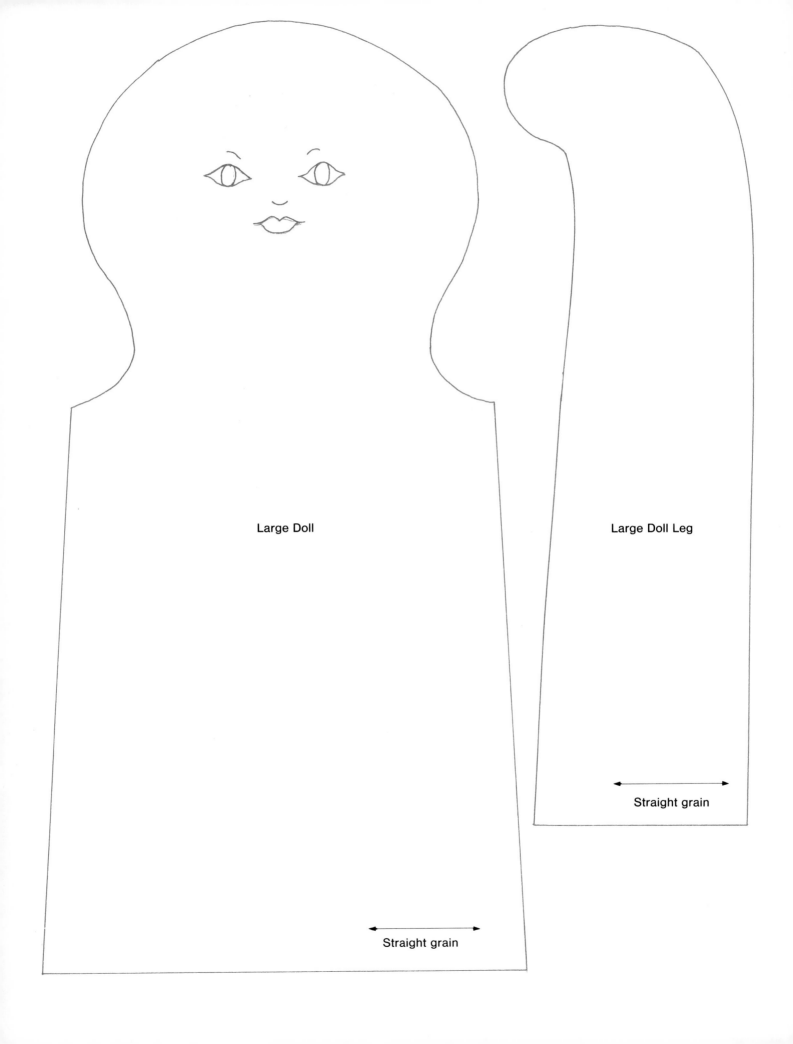

Large Doll

Large Doll Leg

Straight grain

Straight grain

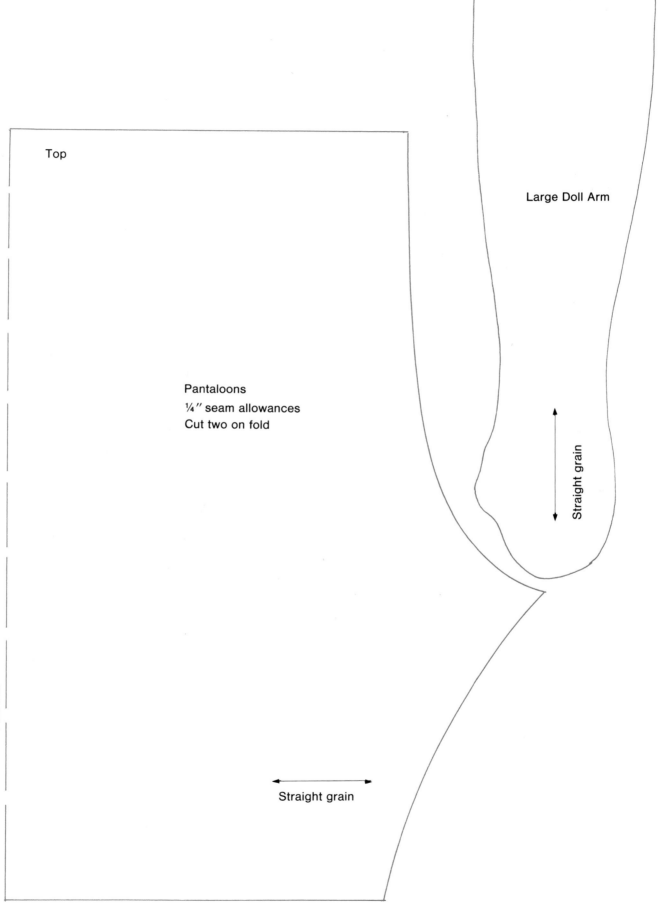

Top

Pantaloons
¼″ seam allowances
Cut two on fold

Large Doll Arm

Straight grain

Fold line

Straight grain

15

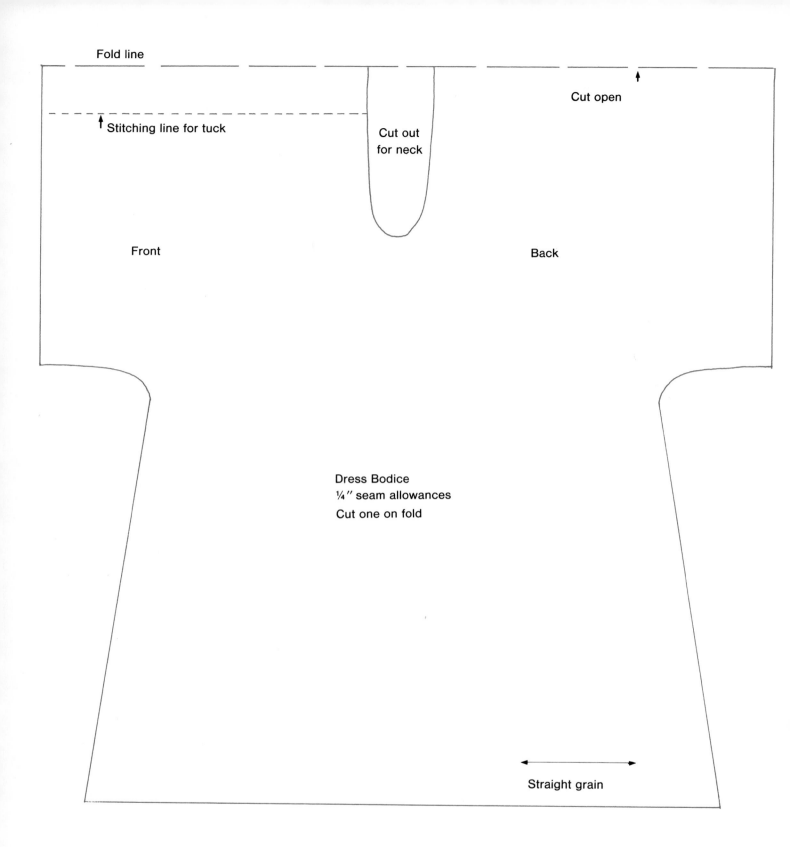

Fold line

Stitching line for tuck

Cut out
for neck

Cut open

Front

Back

Dress Bodice
¼″ seam allowances
Cut one on fold

Straight grain

above the end of the hems. Press the seam open. Run a double row of gathering threads along the top. Turn up and stitch a 1¼″ hem on the skirt of the large doll; 1″ on the small one.

Cut the bodice-sleeve piece, placing it on the fold of the fabric as directed on the pattern piece. Cut open the back on the line shown. Make a ½″ tuck down the center front, stitching on the line shown. Press the tuck flat over the stitching line. Hem each side of the back opening. Make a narrow hem on the sleeve edges.

Reinforce the neck edge by machine-stitching around it a scant ¼″ from the edge. Trim to ⅛″ and clip at the curves. Press the raw edge to the inside on the stitching line. Stitch the hem with two closely spaced rows of machine stitching.

Sew the ⅛″-wide elastic to the sleeve edges about ¼″ inside the hem, stretching the elastic to make the edge gather. Sew underarm and side seams. Press the facings back to the inside.

Pull up the gathers of the skirt to fit the bodice waist and stitch them together. Press. Sew two snaps to the back opening.

Apron If an old handkerchief is being used for the apron, cut across the entire width (usually 10″ to 12″) and make the piece about 5″ long for an apron similar to the ones the dolls are wearing. The apron can also be as long as the dress if the handkerchief is too nice to cut away.

If fabric other than a handkerchief is to be used to make the apron, cut the piece 12″ x 7″. Hem the two short sides and turn up a 1″ hem at the bottom edge.

For either fabric or handkerchief apron cut a strip of muslin 1½″ x 30″ for the band. Gather the apron skirt to a 6″ length and fit it to the middle of the band; stitch them together. Make a very narrow hem on the band, beginning at the point at which the band joins the apron and continuing around the band to the opposite side. Fold the hemmed band over the raw edges at the top of the skirt and stitch it down.

The small doll in the photograph is wearing a fancy collar made from one of the corners cut off its handkerchief apron. The cut edges were simply hemmed and the piece fastened at the neck edge with the stitching for the hem.

Additional antiquing can be added to the dresses after construction, as was done here. Wet the fabric slightly and paint a strong coffee solution along the hems and seams. Apply some in the gathers also. Treat the aprons and pantaloons the same way. Iron dry.

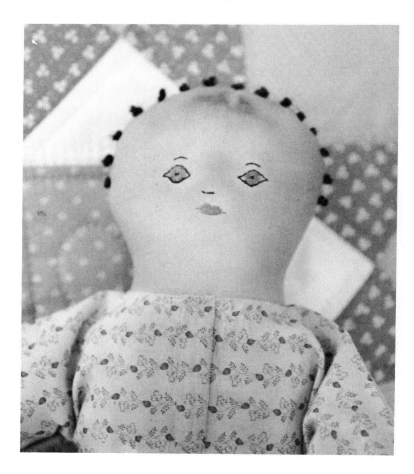

QUILTED PATCHWORK CAT

Plump teddy bears made from quilt fragments; ducks, cats, and amusing piglets cut from coverlet scraps—all these whimsical little creatures find their way into country decorating plans. Some are collected over a period of years; others, like this winsome kitty cat with his perky bow, are made from new materials but fit the country look just as well as their older counterparts. Part of the secret of this cat's easy adjustment to country living is the soft, aged look he gets from treatment with a coffee dye solution.
Size: 12″

MATERIALS

calico and muslin, small scraps, enough to piece a 10″ x 14″ rectangle
fabric for backing—11″ x 15″
quilting fleece—11″ x 15″
quilting thread, off-white
black embroidery floss—1½ yards
fiberfill
quilting needle
heavy tracing paper
plastic for templates
ribbon, ½″ wide—⅝ yard
blue washout pen

INSTRUCTIONS

Since this is a small patchwork project, involving piecing together only enough squares and triangles to make a simple rectangular shape, it is a good candidate for a first venture into this fascinating process. The **Patchwork and Quilting** chapter contains the basic instructions for these procedures and will be very helpful to the novice.

Cut plastic templates for a 2″ square and a triangle using the diagrams with the Quilted Patchwork Heart Pillow. Using the templates, cut enough pieces to assemble into a rectangle 10″ x 16″. (The piece should be made up of five 2″ squares across and eight 2″ squares vertically—actually a mixture of squares and triangles to make forty 2″ squares.)

Assemble the pieces by hand or machine, arranging the colors and shapes into a pleasing random pattern. Press.

Trace the top portion of the cat and the slashed line. Move the tracing paper to the diagram of the lower part of the cat, match the slashed lines, and

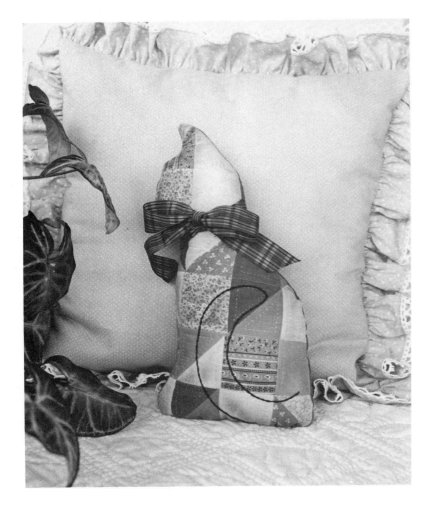

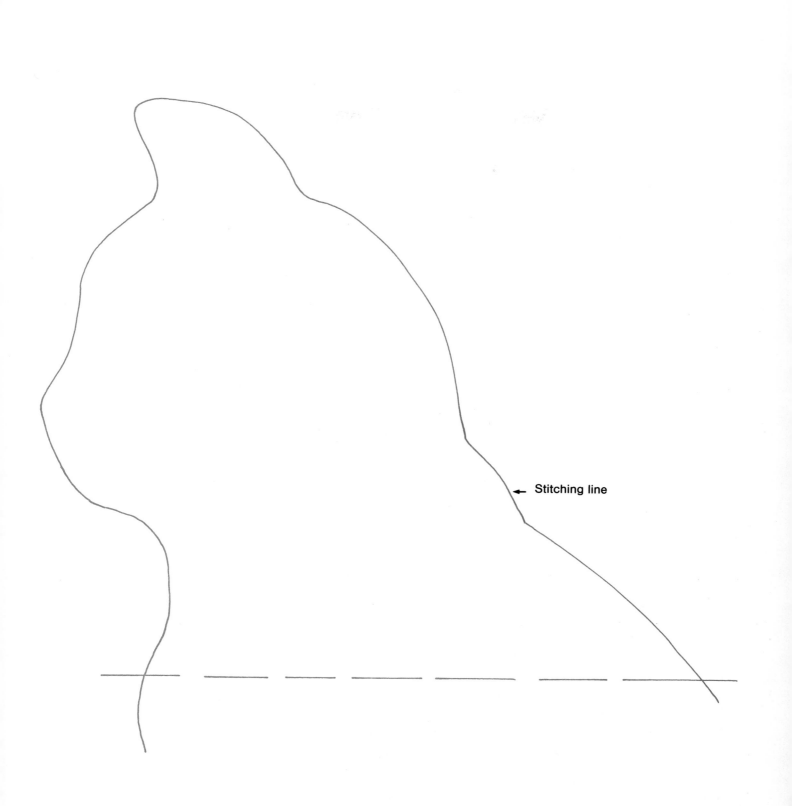

← Stitching line

19

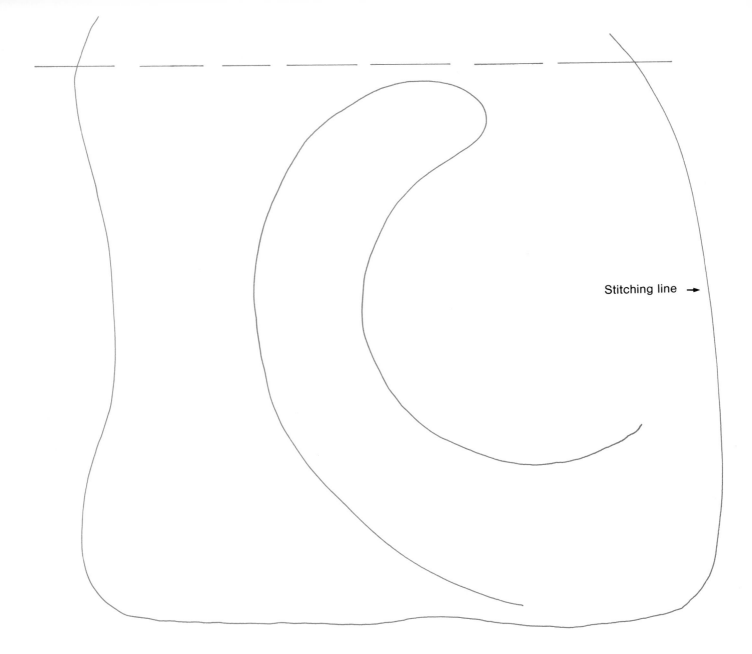

Stitching line →

trace that portion, completing the cat. Cut out the traced cat. Lay it on the right side of the patchwork and trace the outline onto the fabric with a blue washout pen. Draw the tail also.

Using four strands of the black floss, embroider the tail outline using **outline stitch**.

Baste the quilting fleece to the back of the patchwork. **Quilt** ¼″ in-side each seam line, following the seam lines. (Naturally there's no need to quilt any portions of the patchwork that fall outside the cat outline.)

Wet the completed piece and "age" it following the suggestions in

Antiquing Fabrics. Dry it in the clothes dryer and fluff up the quilting.

To reinforce the patchwork, stitch around the cat on the stitching line on the fabric. Place the backing fabric and the patchwork right sides together, and baste or pin. With the patchwork on top and using the reinforcing stitching line as the stitching line, sew the two together, leaving an opening at the bottom for stuffing.

Cut out the cat, trimming the seam to ⅜″. Turn, stuff, and close the opening. Give your cat a big perky bow and find him a sunny windowsill to enjoy!

20

DOLL QUILT

Antique miniature quilts made specifically for dolls are among the most prized and hardest to find. Collectors seek out these rare tiny treasures and willingly pay high prices for the hand-crafted pieces. Although usually made by mothers, grandmothers, and aunts, some of these quilts are thought to have been little girls' first efforts at learning the necessary arts of piecing and quilting.

Many who own old doll quilts use them as wall hangings or display them in various other ways to establish a country atmosphere in their homes. These old ones are fragile and costly and have an aura about them that can't be duplicated, but we can make reproductions that have something of the familiar used look and add the same country feeling to our rooms. New cotton fabrics that copy old calico print designs can be "antiqued" with a coffee solution to help create the look we love.

One of my favorites of the old doll quilt patterns is this heart design, in which the hearts were cut from an assortment of calico scraps and sewn to the individual muslin squares by the appliqué method. Stenciled hearts were substituted in this version, to establish an older look, but the original appliqué method can be used if preferred.

The sizes of the old doll quilts vary greatly, some being only about 12″ square. This pattern can be reduced easily by omitting the borders or miniaturizing the center squares and the hearts themselves. The pattern is also suitable for enlargement to crib size by the addition of more squares to the center field.

Some of the old quilts were made with all the hearts in one color; others used a random assortment of colors and patterns. I used fifteen blue hearts with the surprise of a single gold one as a reminder that folk artists usually used what was on hand. The imaginary designer of this quilt ran out of blue fabric and had to complete the field with the addition of a spark of gold. Actually this happened often and is a charming design statement that tells us much about the early quilt maker.
Size: 28″ x 28″

MATERIALS

muslin—⅝ yard
dark calico print—¾ yard
pale calico print—1 yard
backing—1 yard
batting—approximately 32″ x 32″
quilting thread, off-white

stencil paint: blue, gold—small jars of
   each
stencil film—4½″ x 4½″
stencil brush
stencil knife
watercolor brush
blue washout pen
quilting needle
NOTE: All fabrics should be 100 percent cotton. This sews and takes the
"antiquing" best. The dark calico print
is for the inner border. The one illustrated here is a calico stripe, which
makes a pretty frame for the muslin
field. Any small calico-like print can
be subsituted. The backing may be
either of the calicos or plain muslin.

INSTRUCTIONS

Trace the template pattern onto the
stencil film and cut it out around the
outline. Then cut out the heart shape.

Using the template, outline sixteen
squares on the muslin with a washout
pen. Next, stencil the hearts (do this
before cutting the squares apart as it is
easier to work on the larger piece of
fabric): Center the template on each
square, and following the instructions
on the paint container and the tips in
Stenciling, make fifteen blue hearts
and one gold one, or use another color
arrangement if desired. Set the stencil
color as indicated by the paint manufacturer.

Cut apart the squares. Carefully
stitch them together to form a square
center field. Place the gold heart where
you prefer—mine is in the lower left
corner. All seams in the quilt should
be the standard quilter's ¼″. Press
seams open.

From the dark calico cut two
pieces 16½″ x 2½″ and two pieces 21″

x 2½". Note that the 2½" width of these pieces was determined by the width of the stripes in that particular fabric. It may be necessary to adjust this width for other stripes. If so, adjust also the size of the outer border. For most overall calico prints the 2½" width should be all right.

Sew the 16½" pieces to the top and bottom of the field. Sew the longer pieces to the sides and press the seams open.

From the pale calico print cut two pieces 21" x 5¼" and two pieces 31" x 5¼". Sew the shorter pieces to the top and bottom edges, the longer pieces to the sides, as before. Press the seams open.

Antique the finished top with a coffee or tea solution following the guidelines in **Antiquing Fabrics**: Dampen the top first so the solution bleeds into a soft-edged line where it is used. Using a watercolor brush, paint on the solution along all seam lines and along the unfinished edges of the outer border. Remember that the brown color will be lighter after rinsing and drying. Dip the remainder of the dark calico and the backing fabric in the solution to "age" them also. Rinse well and iron dry.

Cut the batting and the backing fabric to the size of the assembled top. Lay the quilt top on a flat surface with the wrong side up. Position the batting on top. Add the backing, right side up. Carefully pin all layers together and baste firmly to prevent shifting.

Start **quilting** on the center field and work to the outer edges. Quilt around each stenciled heart and on each seam joining the squares. Run another row of quilting stitches ¼" inside each outlined square.

Quilt each seam line joining the borders and run a diagonal line of stitches from the inside corner of the first border to the outer corner of the quilt. Quilt on the lines of the inner border stripes, or if you are using a printed calico, run two parallel rows through the center of the border.

Cut 1½"-wide bias strips from the "aged" inner border fabric, piecing them to make a length that reaches around the outside edge. Press the seams open. Use the bias to bind the quilt edges, mitering the corners as necessary. Quilt an outline ¼" inside the binding seam.

Consider adding an inscription noting for whom the quilt was made, by whom, and the date—in your own script—to the back before assembling. Embroider with tiny **back stitches** in slightly contrasting thread. If not the whole inscription, at least add the date. You'll be surprised how much these touches mean in later years.

QUILTED PATCHWORK HEART PILLOW

Clothing, pillows, stuffed animals, and all manner of folk art objects made from old quilts are currently very fashionable, but a true quilt lover would never cut up an old quilt, no matter how tattered, to make it up into these whimsies. One can use fragments of no value or scraps of old quilts that were never assembled, but it is just as easy to piece and "antique" new materials for this use. This process is so quick and easy that a few hours at the sewing machine or an evening piecing by hand will yield enough patchwork for several pillows.

These are not heirlooms, but perhaps it is too soon to disclaim them, for certainly most of the folk art we collect so avidly today was not intended as heirloom material when it was made.

Two-inch squares and triangles that form a 2" square when two are sewn together are the ideal "patches" for these projects. Use an assortment of scraps of cotton calico and unbleached muslin and combine them randomly to make a piece of fabric large enough to contain the design. Quilt in lines following the seam lines

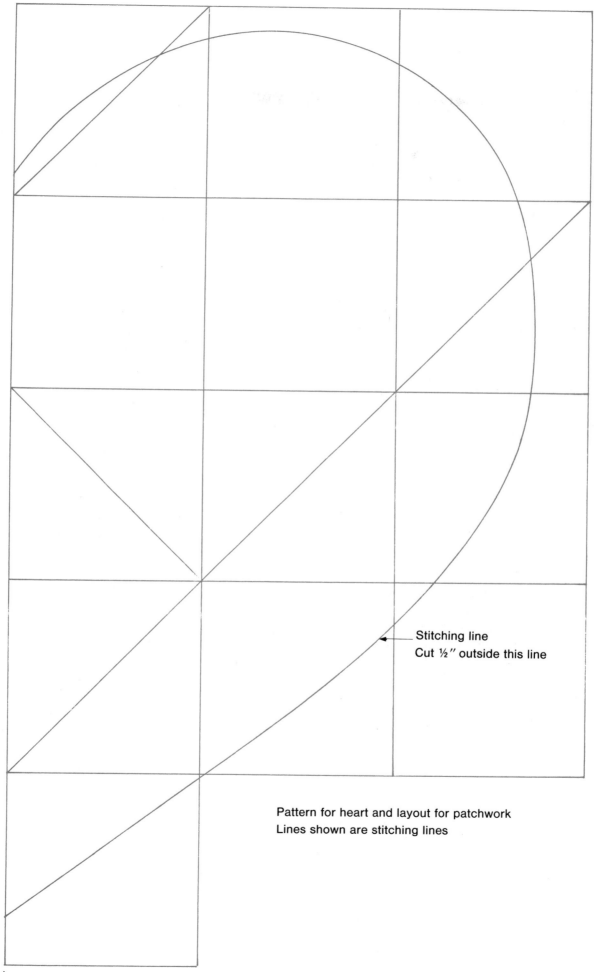

Stitching line
Cut ½″ outside this line

Pattern for heart and layout for patchwork
Lines shown are stitching lines

Center line

and antique with coffee or tea before assembling.

This little heart pillow with double lace-edged ruffles has a special charm of its own and should find a home in any country room. It would make a lovely gift—especially as a valentine!

Size: 9″ x 10½″ excluding ruffle

MATERIALS

scraps of calico and muslin to cut twenty-six 2″ squares
muslin for backing and ruffle—½ yard
heavy cotton lace, ecru, ½″ wide—5 yards
quilting fleece—12″ x 12″
quilting thread, off-white
quilting needle
heavy tracing paper
watercolor brush
washout pen
plastic for templates
fiberfill

INSTRUCTIONS

Basic quilting and piecing directions are given in **Patchwork and Quilting**. Before beginning to cut out the patches, you may want to check that chapter to decide whether you prefer to cut plastic templates without seam allowances or with them as shown on the accompanying charts.

Cut enough squares and triangles to assemble into a piece which is six squares wide and four squares deep with two additional squares attached at the center of the lower edge, as shown on the drawing. Copy the layout of squares and triangles shown on the chart or simply arrange yours in a pleasing pattern. Placement of color for balance is more important than the actual arrangement of the pieces.

Assemble the pieces either by hand or with machine stitching, using care to match the corners of the

squares. Draw the outline of the heart on the assembled patchwork piece. An easy way to do this is to trace the heart on heavy paper, then cut it out and trace around the edges right onto the patchwork with a washout pen. Do not cut out the patchwork heart until after quilting and antiquing have been completed.

Pin the square of quilting fleece to the back of the patchwork and baste them together to prevent shifting during the quilting. **Quilt** ¼″ inside each little piece, following the seam lines. There is no need to quilt any portion of the fabric that falls outside the heart outline.

Wet the piece. Antique with coffee or tea solution following the tips in **Antiquing Fabrics**. Experiment with the dye solution in one of the portions of fabric outside the outline to get the feel of the process. I like to use a watercolor brush and paint along all the seam lines, letting the dye bleed into the fabric in a soft line. Some squares I give a thorough soaking with the solution so the overall look will be rather uneven. A quick spin in the dryer will make the patchwork look great—it fluffs it up and sets the dye. Cut out the heart ½″ *outside* the outline.

Dip the backing and ruffle fabric in the solution also. Rinse them and iron them dry.

From the muslin cut two strips 3″ wide and two strips 2½″ wide across the full 45″ width of the fabric. Seam the two 3″ pieces to make a continuous length. Hem one edge and sew lace to it without gathering the lace. Make the narrower ruffle in the same manner. With the raw edges together and both right sides facing up, run two gathering threads around the strip ½″ from the raw edge. Pull up the gathering threads to make the ruffle fit the outside edge of the heart. With right sides together, sew the ruffle to the edge of the heart on the stitching line.

Place the heart on top of the muslin, wrong side up, and pin the two together. Baste and stitch the two together using the stitching line from the ruffle as a guideline and leaving an opening on one side for stuffing.

Trim the backing fabric to the heart shape. Turn. Stuff the pillow and close the opening.

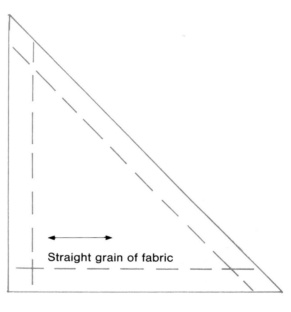

Straight grain of fabric

Templates

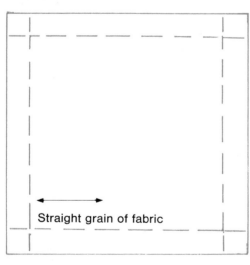

Straight grain of fabric

Solid lines are cutting lines
Stitch on broken lines to form 2″ squares

ANGEL GABRIEL QUILTED PILLOW

Gabriel with his horn stenciled on unbleached muslin and quilted makes a cute, quick pillow, but the design will adapt just as well to a tote bag, apron, towel, toaster cover, curtain border, or other household use.

Size: 11″ x 14″ excluding ruffle

MATERIALS

unbleached muslin—15″ x 19″, two pieces
quilting fleece—15″ x 19″
printed fabric for back and ruffle—⅝ yard
stencil paints: blue, green, brown, gold, fleshtone—small jars of each
stencil film
fiberfill
blue washout pen
stencil knife
stencil brush
quilting needle

INSTRUCTIONS

Using the drawing on the facing page, trace a master stencil and cut it out along the oval outline. Cut away the hair, robe border, and sleeve border on the master. On another piece of film cut out the wing, face, hand, and foot. From a third cut the trumpet and main portion of the robe. To save having to

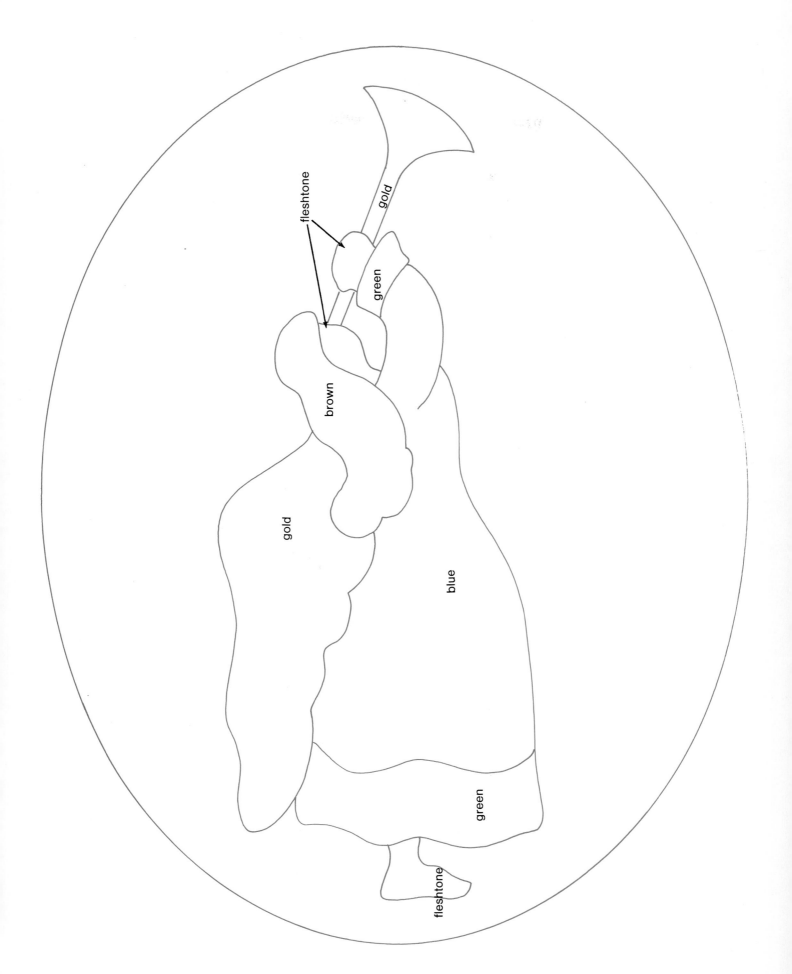

29

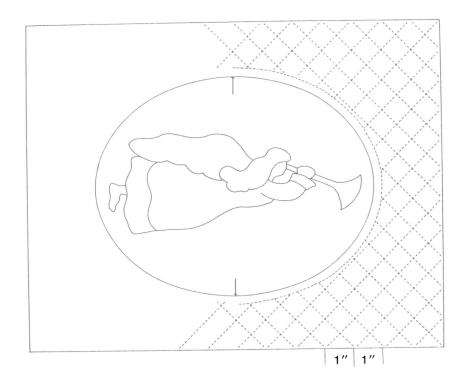

1" 1"

use another piece of film, move closer to the edge and cut the opening for the sleeve.

Mark the outline of an 11" x 14" rectangle on one piece of muslin. Center the oval master stencil on the rectangle and with a blue washout pen trace the oval.

Following the tips in **Stenciling** and the directions on your paints, stencil the angel using the suggested colors or a palette of your own choosing.

Then place the oval master stencil over the angel, matching the shape of the oval to the blue outline. With light circular strokes, paint the background of the rectangle blue, shading it darker at the edges of the oval and at the outside edges of the rectangle. Set the stencil color according to manufacturer's instructions.

Use the washout pen to mark quilting lines on the blue section, as shown in the drawing. Place marks at 1" intervals around the outside edges of the rectangle. Draw lines connecting the marks to form the diamond quilting pattern.

Sandwich the quilting fleece between the stenciled piece and the other piece of muslin. Pin and baste the three layers together to prevent shifting during quilting.

Quilt all outlines of the angel. Quilt around the oval on the line where the blue begins, and quilt another line around the oval ¼" outside the first, on the blue. Quilt the diamond pattern.

Wipe away any visible marking lines. Make up the pillow with a ruffle as shown or tailor it to fit your needs (see **Pillow Construction**).

OHIO STAR QUILTED PILLOW

The names of pieced quilt patterns, their roots and variations, can become an engrossing study for they are linked inextricably to the history of the regions in which they originated and to the people who created them. Many are known by five or six different but equally valid names; some are very descriptive or humorous, others are romantic, and still others give us a key to events shaping the period in which the pattern was developed.

This particular design is most commonly known as the Ohio Star or the Variable Star, but it is also often called Texas Star, Lone Star, Flying Crows, Eight Point Star, and Happy Home. Subtle variations in the geometric arrangements change the design and create others with equally descriptive and interesting names.

A very popular pattern among quilt makers, the Ohio Star is easy enough to be an ideal choice for the beginning quilter but challenging enough to be a favorite for any skill level. Although shown here as a pillow top, the square can also be joined to others, as was traditionally done, to make a bed-size quilt. Consider also using three squares joined for a table runner, or nine in a square for a small wall hanging. Single squares can be used to upholster small stools and chair seats. By shaping the framing pieces, one can fashion an attractive chair seat with either a tailored or a ruffled finish. Single squares also make generous placemats. Nothing could be more "country" than these accessories. *Size: 16″ x 16″ excluding ruffle*

MATERIALS

fabric—½ yard each of three contrasting or blending prints; ¾ yard of another print which will also be used for pillow back and ruffle (see note below)
muslin—17″ x 17″
batting—17″ x 17″
sewing thread to match fabric
quilting thread, off-white or white
quilting and sewing needles
lace—3½ yards
quilt template, plastic or cardboard
washout pen
fiberfill
NOTE: The piece shown was made from an assortment of three blues and plain white. The three blues are shades of one family. One is a pale shade with a tiny white pin dot, one is a slightly deeper tone with a small leaf print. The darkest one has a larger

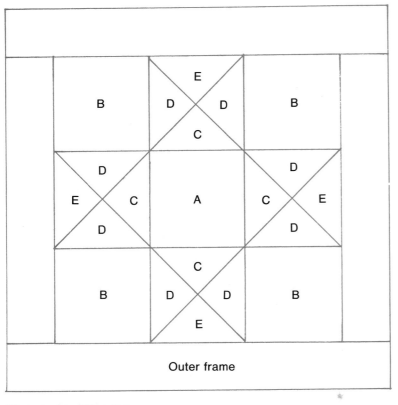

Outer frame

Diagram for pillow top

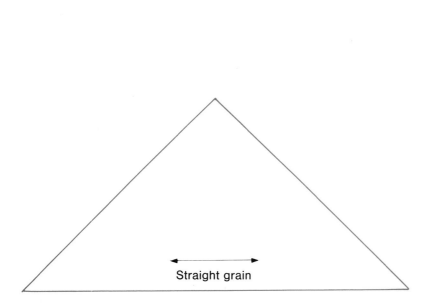

Straight grain

Template for triangles

To make the 16″ pillow shown, use this template for the triangles and the 4″ square template for the doll quilt on page 22, omitting the seam allowances on the square as noted in the instructions.

stylized floral and leaf print in white. This combination makes up into a softly subtle block. Other mixtures will create vastly different effects and are really fun to try. The design can be made from two, three, or four prints or solids, the key being to use one print only for the background pieces (B and E on the layout).

Many quilt shops have a precut piece of fabric which they call a "Quilter's Sample," "Fat Quarter," or various other names of their own devising. These are four 18″ x 22½″ pieces (¼ yard) cut from a full yard of 45″-wide material. This is a very handy size for small projects since it cuts to much better advantage than the standard ¼ yard cut straight across the 45″ width of the fabric. If this quilter's cut of fabric is available, three of these plus the ¾ yard for the backing and ruffle will make this pillow.

INSTRUCTIONS

Using the stencil pattern for the Doll Quilt on page 22, cut a 4″ square template without seam allowances. Also cut a triangular template following the pattern here.

Using the templates and allowing for ¼″ seam allowances as discussed in **Patchwork and Quilting,** cut the following pieces to correspond to the pieces letter-keyed on the drawing: center square A, one 4″ square; corner square B, four 4" squares; inner triangles C, four triangles; star points D, eight triangles; outer triangles E, four triangles.

Lay the pieces on a flat surface, placing them as they will be when assembled. Change anything you don't like. Very little material is involved at this point and sometimes patterns or colors react to each other in unexpected ways, so it is better to rearrange them than to proceed with something you don't feel happy about.

Using the piecing tips on page 135, assemble the square. Press well. The finished square is 12" plus the seam allowance on all outside edges.

From the fabric that is to be the outer frame, tear two strips 2½" x 12½" and two strips 2½" x 16". Stitch the two shorter pieces to the top and bottom of the square. Then stitch the longer pair to the side edges to make a 16" square.

On heavy tracing paper or template plastic, trace the heart shape from the stencil for the Doll Quilt on page 22 and cut it out. Center it on each of the five square blocks of the finished top and trace around it with a washout pen or pencil to provide a quilting guide.

Lay the muslin backing flat, place the batting on top, then the pieced top over that with the right side up. Pin all three layers together. Baste with long stitches to prevent shifting during the quilting.

Small pieces like this may be **quilted** in the hand or in a hoop or frame. Traditionally these geometrics are quilted ¼" inside all the joining lines. Quilt also around each heart outline, and place another row of stitching ¼" outside the seam joining the square to the outer frame.

When the quilting is finished, cut a piece of fabric for the pillow back and from the remainder make enough ruffling for the outside edge. To make the ruffle, cut enough 3"-wide strips on the straight grain of the fabric to measure approximately 3½ yards. Join the strips to make one continuous piece. Hem one edge and sew lace to that edge. Stitch a double row of gathering stitches near the raw edge, and gather to fit the outside edge of the pillow top. Pin and baste in place, allowing extra fullness at the corners.

With right sides together, join the pillow top to the back, leaving an opening at the bottom for stuffing. Trim the seam and corners. Turn, stuff, and close the opening.

AUTUMN LEAVES PATCHWORK HANGING

Lovers of patchwork will recognize this pieced design as the favorite Autumn Leaves quilt block—with the slight alteration of the addition of an appliquéd goose and a yellow frame on the central square. Though the pattern is traditionally used alone, this combination of precise geometric patchwork with natural forms that can be appliquéd opens all kinds of possibilities for quilted projects. Many of the quilt block designs can be adapted this way. It would be fun to add bears to Bear Paw, a New England church to Evening Star, a basket of flowers to Hands All 'Round, a bunny in the center of Snow Crystals, flowers or berries to any of the basket designs.
Size: 19" x 19"

MATERIALS

cotton fabric
    dark blue small print—1 yard
    bright yellow—½ yard
    white—¼ yard
quilting fleece—19½" x 19½"
fusable interfacing—7" x 5"
quilting thread, white
embroidery floss: white, orange, gray,
    black—very small amounts of each
fabric marking pen, orange
quilting needle

INSTRUCTIONS

If you have never pieced a quilt square, see the general instructions in **Patchwork and Quilting** for tips about buying fabric, washing it prior to cutting, making a template, and cutting and piecing.

    From the blue print fabric cut one piece 20" x 20" for the back of the hanging. Using the templates for the Quilted Patchwork Heart Pillow, also cut twelve squares, sixteen triangles, one square 6½" x 6½", and four rectangles 2½" x 14½".

    Next, use the template to cut sixteen white squares.

    From the yellow material, cut on the true bias enough 4"-wide strips to piece together a strip 82" long. From the remainder of the fabric cut sixteen yellow triangles and four strips 2" x 6½".

    If this were the unaltered Autumn Leaves quilt square, the center (6½") square would be pieced from nine smaller squares containing the stems of the leaves. Since it is to be ornamented instead with the goose appliqué, it is better to cut it from one piece as directed. The chart shows the layout of the pattern pieces, and one can easily see that the fastest way to put it together would be to piece in horizontal rows, joining the consecutive rows as is usually done.

I find it easier to make a neat center square if I appliqué the yellow frame to the blue 6½" square before it is assembled into the piece—but if you prefer, it may be appliquéd in the traditional manner after the piece is put together.

To make the frame, fold the yellow 2" x 6½" strips in half lengthwise. With the raw edges together, baste the strips to the sides of the blue square, folding at each corner to form a miter. Stitch the folded edges down with tiny invisible stitches. (The fabric is doubled to prevent the blue from showing through the yellow.)

Piece rows 1 and 2 and join them. Then piece the side sections of rows 3, 4, and 5. Join the side sections to the center square. Piece rows 6 and 7; join them to the bottom of the incomplete square. Finally add the navy rectangles and white squares which form the outer border.

Finish piecing the entire square.

Trace the goose design and transfer it to the white fabric (see page 114). Embroider the eye with a single strand of black floss and tiny **back stitches.** Embroider the line at the top of the beak with orange **outline stitch,** using three strands of floss. Work the wing and feather lines with outline stitch and three strands of gray floss. Color the beak and feet with the permanent orange marker.

Fuse the goose to lightweight fusable interfacing. With white thread machine-stitch around the outline of the goose, using a short stitch just inside the transfer line. Carefully cut out the goose on the transfer line.

Place the goose in the position shown on the drawing. Baste it in place, or use a small amount of glue-stick if you prefer. Using white for the body and orange for the bill and feet, work a row of **buttonhole stitch** around the figure, using a single strand of floss and placing the stitches close together so the raw edge is completely covered. This method of appliqué allows for much more intricate shapes than the traditional folded-under finish.

Sandwich the quilting fleece between the finished top and the backing piece, making sure that the larger

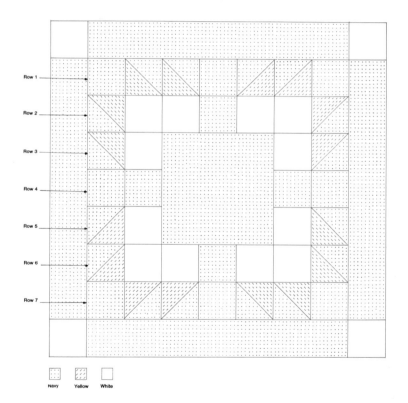

Shown without the appliquéd duck and yellow frame, this is the piecing diagram for the hanging. Following the written instructions, join first the seven rows of the large square, then add the four white corners and the four navy oblongs that make the outer border.

↑ Cutting line

pieces of fleece and backing fabric extend evenly all around. Pin and baste the three layers together. **Quilt** ¼″ inside the stitching lines of all the triangles and all the squares except the four white ones at the outside corners. Quilt around both edges of the yellow frame and around the goose. Leave the blue rectangles and the four corner squares until after the piece is bound.

Trim the edges of the assembled piece to even them. The backing and fleece should extend ¼″ beyond the pieced top on all sides.

Bind the edges with the yellow bias strips, stitching them in a ½″ seam. Finish quilting by putting in the rows on the blue rectangles and the white corner squares.

Make three thread loops on the top back to use for hanging the piece. These will be invisible. Or if you prefer, three fabric loops (yellow) can be made to fit over a decorative rod.

BUNNY COUNTRY CRIB QUILT

One of my great-grandmothers, Sarah James, followed the lovely tradition of making each of her babies a pieced quilt before it was born. She was an expert needlewoman and favored patterns composed of many tiny curved pieces—difficult to put together but beautiful when finished. I have been fortunate to inherit the quilt she made for my grandfather, and I prize it because of both its history and the exceptional workmanship. Once scarlet, dark green, and white, it is now wine, brown, and off-white, but the beautiful fabric is without a sign of wear although my grandfather told me it was always on his bed until he outgrew it (it is sized for a short trundle bed).

If you'd like to make a quilt for one of your babies, here is a pattern that you can finish in a lot less time than the ten years it took me to finish mine! The country look is appropriate for most nurseries and the bunny pattern is appealing. It's nice also to make a matching dust ruffle for the crib, using more of the backing fabric.

When choosing fabric, look for a tightly woven all-cotton muslin. For the ruffle, backing, and the lattice trim, choose cotton in a small print (cottons wear better than clothing blends of cotton and polyester, and match the muslin in weight and texture to make a handsome quilt).

The fabric chosen for the pictured quilt is a cotton check for the lattice strips and ruffle, and a coordinating check with a large windowpane overcheck for the back. Any combination of prints is possible. Try also one print fabric with a matching or contrasting plain one, or make both back and front all one color or print.

Tying the main color of the fabric to the color of the stenciled hearts is the key to a successful combination.
Size: 58″ x 45″ excluding ruffle

MATERIALS

muslin—1¼ yards
print fabric—5½ yards
stencil paints: pink, brown, soft
   green—small jar of each
stencil film
fabric marking pen, brown
batting—crib size
tracing paper
stencil knife
stencil brush
quilting thread
quilting needle

INSTRUCTIONS

Wash and iron both fabrics before cutting. Treat them the way the finished quilt will be, so if there is going to be any shrinkage it is taken care of before assembly.

The drawing shows a little more than a quarter of the border design and the entire bunny placed as it should be on the 12" square. To make a complete pattern, first draw a 12" square on tracing paper. Then trace this portion of the design onto it, matching the outlines of the two squares. Fold the tracing paper into quarters and trace the remainder of the border (see pages 139–140).

Cut a 12" square of stencil film for the master stencil and trace the entire design onto it. Cut out the four hearts, the flower bud (#7), and the bunny—except for his right ear and his tail.

On another 12" square of film, trace and cut out the right ear, the tail, and the leaves numbered 1 through 6. Also cut out the inner ear (#8) and the eye. On a small scrap of film, cut out leaves #9 and #10, placing them far enough apart so they can be used separately without smearing the paint.

Save the bunny shape cut out from the master stencil to use for defining the lines at his sides. I cut the body apart along the dotted lines on the chart; then after the body has been stenciled, before the master stencil is removed, I hold these pieces in place and work over them at the sides to define those short lines.

A 3" square stencil is needed for the small muslin squares. Trace the small heart onto the stencil, centered, and cut it out.

In planning the stencil colors, use a minimum number for the best results. Try to match the hearts and flower buds to the predominant color in the lattice strips and ruffle. The brown bunny and soft green leaves will probably coordinate with most fabrics.

Mark the muslin carefully into twelve 12" squares, taking care that the lines are on the straight grain of the fabric. Cut these apart. Also mark and cut out six 3" muslin squares.

For the most even results, **stencil** all of one color on all the squares, then proceed to the next color.

Begin with the master stencil. Line the edges up with the edges of the muslin square to center the design. Do all the hearts and buds. Place the heaviest color along the edges of the cutouts so a shaded effect is achieved. While you are using the pink paint, stencil the little hearts on the small squares.

Next stencil the leaves (#1 through #6), shading most heavily at the bottoms. While the green paint is still on the brush, hold the cutout for leaf #9 in place and stencil that. Then do leaf #10. Make the tops of these two darkest, to separate them from the other leaves.

Using the master stencil again, paint the bunny brown. Work over the entire body lightly in a circular motion, then concentrate on the edges to make them darker. Before removing the stencil, insert the cut-apart body sections one at a time and darken the contours of the body along the short solid lines at the sides.

Color in the right ear and the tail, making the tail dark around the edges with a light center. Apply the brown to the ear in the same manner, leaving most of the inner portion untinted. Then put pink in the inner ear. If the tail and body seem to blend into each other, put the master stencil in place and work over the body where it joins the tail to redefine the line.

Layout

Set the paint according to the directions on the label. Press the squares. Using the permanent brown marker and the stencil as a guide, draw the eyes.

From the print fabric, cut the following pieces:

quilt back—45″ x 60″
two pieces 5″ x 38″
two pieces 5″ x 60″
seventeen pieces 3″ x 12″
ruffle—eight strips 7″ wide across the full 45″ width of the fabric

Assemble the quilt top, following the layout. Match the corners of the pieces carefully. Trim seams to ¼″ and press them toward the darker fabric.

Make the ruffle by joining the ends of the 7″ strips to make a continuous piece. Press the seams open. With the seams inside, fold the ruffle in half lengthwise to make a 3½″-wide piece. Gather along the raw edges and pull up to fit the outside of the quilt top. Pin the ruffle in place and machine-baste.

With the right sides facing, stitch the top and back together, leaving the bottom edge open for turning. Trim the seam. Lay the quilt on a flat surface and place the batting on top. With very large loose stitches, baste the batting to the top and side edges, just to hold it in place when the quilt is turned. Trim away any excess batting along the edges.

Carefully turn the quilt right side out. Lay it on a flat surface and baste the three layers together to keep them from shifting. Baste the bottom edge closed and then stitch it with small invisible stitches.

Quilt as follows:

Bunny squares: Quilt around bunny and on all lines outlining the tail, eye, and inner ear. Outline also the hearts, leaves, and buds. Work a row of quilting stitches around the square, placing the row ¼″ inside the seam line.

Small muslin squares: Outline the heart and quilt ¼″ inside the seam line.

Inner lattice pieces: Quilt ¼″ inside the seams.

Also quilt ¼″ inside the seam lines of the four large outside lattice pieces, stitching on the sides bordering the muslin only. Finally quilt one line 1″ from the outside edge all the way around the quilt.

Small heart

TRAPUNTO TULIP PILLOW

Although it was not my intention to create a Pennsylvania Dutch design, there is something about this pillow that recalls for me old painted blanket chests made in Berks and Lancaster counties during the middle of the nineteenth century. On many of them the painted colors have mellowed to a soft patina that lends a grace and charm found nowhere else.

Trapunto quilting gives an added depth to the traditional tulip design, and the painted fabric gives the impression of difficult appliqué work without the time-consuming effort usually involved. Sometimes called Italian or stuffed quilting, the trapunto technique adds interest through the addition of extra stuffing in selected areas.

An intriguing new paint was used to tint the designs for this pillow and the pineapple in the next project. Called an "iron-on" dye, the color is painted onto tracing paper or parchment, then applied to the fabric with a hot iron, just like an embroidery transfer. First results may be a little uneven, so a few test designs are needed, but the overall procedure is basically easy and the softness of the color transfer is so lovely that it is worth trying. The look is one that definitely fits the country idiom.

Stencilers may prefer to use the design as a stenciled one, so instructions for both follow. Fabric requirements are different for each type of paint (see note).

Size: 14" x 14"

MATERIALS

muslin, 45" wide—¾ yard (see note)
iron-on paint or stencil paint: deep
    pink, light pink, dark green, light
    green—small amount of each
quilting thread
quilting fleece—16" x 16"
fiberfill
piping cord, pink—3¼ yards
heavy cord—16"
heavy tracing paper
washout pen
stencil film
stencil knife
stencil brush
quilting needle

INSTRUCTIONS

NOTE: Check the label of the iron-on paint for fabric requirements. Most work only on synthetic or synthetic blend fabrics, but some of these are made to look enough like cotton muslin to be appropriate for the country

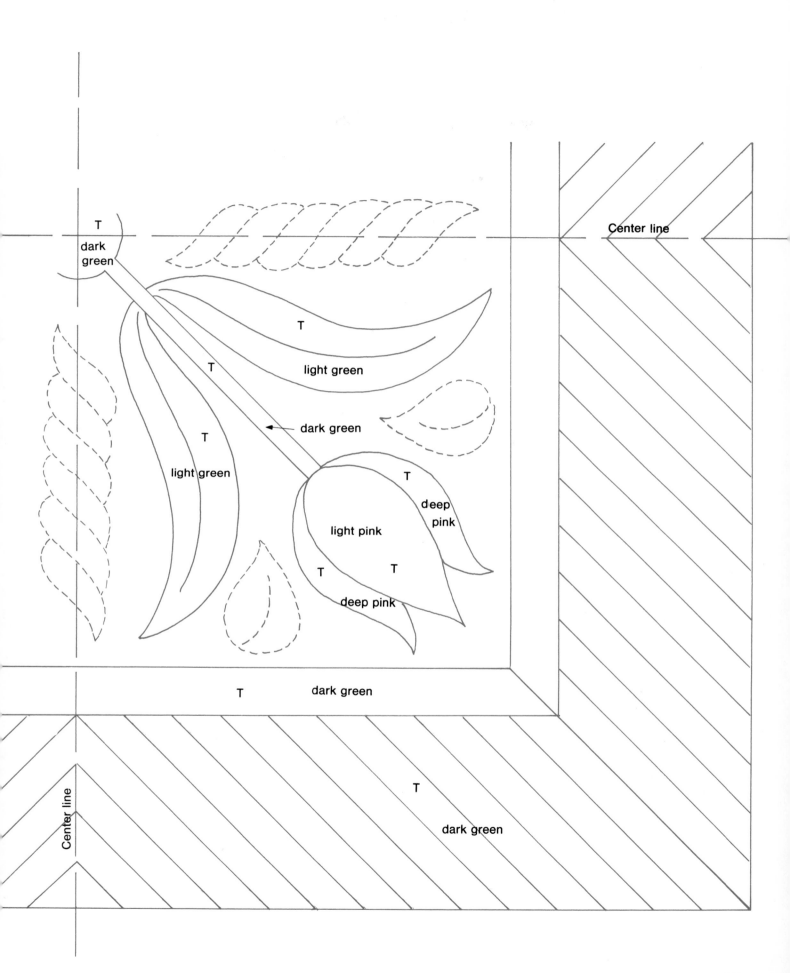

T
dark
green

Center line

T

light green

dark green

T

T

light green

T

deep
pink

light pink

T

T

deep pink

T   dark green

Center line

T

dark green

43

style. As usual use all cotton for stenciling.

From the muslin cut two 16" squares, one strip 3" wide across the full 45" width of the fabric, plus another 3" strip 13" long. Join the two strips to make a 58" boxing piece for the pillow.

Make a full-size drawing of the design on heavy tracing paper by repeating the quarter section shown. The dotted lines on the interior square and the slanted lines in the border are for quilting only and need not be copied on the drawing.

Iron-on Paint Procedure
Placing the colors as shown on the drawing and following the instructions on the paint label, paint the design on tracing paper. Transfer it to one of the fabric squares and follow directions for setting the color.

Note that the drawing is 14" square while the muslin is 16". Paint only inside the 14" square. The surplus fabric will be trimmed away during construction of the pillow.

Stencil Procedure
Cut out the entire design rather than trying to use one quarter of the design and rotating the stencil. Make two 10" square stencils. From the first square cut out the leaves and the light pink center sections of the flowers. From the second stencil cut the deeper pink outside petals of the tulips and the stems, including the circular center.

When **stenciling,** begin with the first stencil and work the paint so it is darker at the edges of the motifs. Treat each leaf as a single motif, leaving the center lighter; the vein line will be added later with a row of quilting. Make the side petals of the flowers a

little darker at the bases than at the tips. While this stencil is in place, use the straight edges and color the outside border to the edge of the 14" square. Set the paint according to the instructions on the label.

After completing painting in either method, mark the quilting lines as shown by the dotted lines on the drawing. Mark also the veins in the leaves, the inner border, and the slanted lines in the outer border.

Baste the pillow top and the quilting fleece together. **Quilt** around the tulips, leaves, and stems. Make a vein in each leaf with a row of quilting stitches. Also quilt the eight small leaves and the four scrolls shown by the dotted lines. Quilt along all the solid lines in the border, ending the slanted lines at the edge of the 14" square.

When quilting is completed, add the trapunto accents: Carefully cut the fleece and insert a small amount of extra stuffing behind the areas marked *T* on the drawing. Use small amounts of fiberfill and push it into place with a crochet hook or other blunt tool. Pull the opening in the fleece together with loose stitches.

To pad the stems, make a small opening in the fleece at the base of the tulip, thread a heavy cord into a large rug or tapestry needle, and pull the cord through the stem. Cut off the ends of the cord, allowing a ½" tail at each end.

Trim the finished pillow top to a 15" square. Using the pink piping cord in the seams, construct a 14" box pillow (see **Pillow Construction**). Stuff with fiberfill.

TRAPUNTO PINEAPPLE PILLOW

Beloved by early Americans and eventually adopted as our traditional symbol of hospitality, the pineapple makes a wonderful design for quilting and stenciling. This version was rendered in a new iron-on paint which makes putting a design on fabric as easy as filling in a child's coloring book. The soft pastel colors fit beautifully into a contemporary country interior.

As in the Trapunto Tulip design, small areas of this pineapple have been accented with stuffing in the quilted portions, thus puffing them more prominently than in the standard wadded quilting. The simplicity of the pineapple motif makes it ideal for this treatment, but it is such a popular symbol that the drawing should be considered for other applications as well. It would be perfect on a hooked rug with the word "Welcome" or your family name—or both—added. A plain border is all that would be needed to finish an attractive rug.

Instructions are given here for using the iron-on paint, but stencil directions are also included so the pillow can be made that way if you prefer.
Size: 14" x 14" excluding ruffle

MATERIALS

muslin, 45" wide—1 yard (see note on
    page 42 about fabric for iron-on or
    stencil paint)
iron-on paint or stencil paints: gold,
    green—small amounts of each
quilting thread
quilting fleece—16" x 16"
fiberfill
washout pen
stencil film
stencil knife
quilting needle

INSTRUCTIONS

Since the border used for this pillow is exactly like the one in the Trapunto Tulip Pillow, it has not been repeated here. Copy the border for the tulip pillow on tracing paper, repeating the quarter shown to make the complete 14" square. Note that on the two drawings of the pineapple there are pairs of parallel lines at the top and bottom plus lines indicating the center of the design. Trace the pineapple within the border, placing it so that the lines at the top and bottom match those of the inner border and the center marks line up. Parts of the leaves extend into the border at both top and bottom.

The vein lines on the leaves are an option, to be used if the pillow is made without the trapunto accents or if the design is used for another purpose.

From the muslin cut two 16"
squares. The balance of the fabric will
make the ruffle.

Iron-on Paint Procedure
Working on the completed tracing,
paint all the leaves green and all the
pineapple sections gold. Flat color is
fine; quilting and the added dimension
of the trapunto provide all the shading
needed.

Following the instructions on the
paint container, transfer the design to
the fabric, centering it on the 16"
square of muslin. Set the color as
directed.

Stencil Procedure
Cut two stencils. Trace the leaves onto
a 14" square of film and cut them out.
Save the cutouts to use as masks in the
places where the leaves extend into the
gold border. The pineapple itself may
be on a smaller piece of acetate film,
so long as reference leaves are shown
top and bottom as an aid in placement.

Stencil the leaves, working in a
little more color at the bases and edges
if a little shading is desired. Put the
pineapple in place and stencil it.

Use the straight edges of a piece
of film as a mask—the leaf stencil is
suitable—and work gold paint in to
make a solid border. In the places
where a leaf extends into the border,
hold the matching cut leaf cutout over
the leaf to shield it from the gold
paint. (Ordinarily on a larger project
where this would have to be repeated
more times, it would be better to cut a
complete stencil for masking, but on a
little job like this I find this a perfectly
satisfactory time-saving method.)

Set the stencil paint according to
instructions on the label.

After completing the tinting of the
fabric, mark the quilting lines. These
are shown by the two lines outlining
the inner border and by the slanting
lines on the outer border. Do not mark
the leaf veins.

Baste the pillow top and the quilting fleece together. **Quilt** around each
section of the pineapple and around
each leaf. Stitch around the inner border on the two parallel lines. Finish the
border by quilting on the slanted lines,
ending the stitching at the edges of the
14" square.

Center line

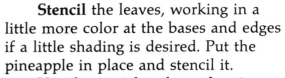

The vein lines for the leaves are
shown in case the design is to be
worked without trapunto accents
or used for another purpose. Do
not copy them if your pillow is to
be made like pictured model.

Add the trapunto accents to each leaf and each section of the pineapple: Cutting carefully, make a small opening in the fleece at the back of each quilted detail. Insert a small amount of fiberfill into the space between the fleece and the muslin, pushing it into place with a crochet hook or other blunt tool. Close the openings by pulling the fleece edges together and holding them with long stitches. It will be necessary to make several openings in the inner border to fill it evenly.

As noted above, the veins of the leaves are shown on the drawing should you wish to finish the design as a more usual wadded-quilting piece. In this case the lines should be quilted.

Trim the finished pillow top to 15″, allowing a ½″ unworked border all around to be used for seam allowance. Cut the remaining muslin and piece as necessary to make a ruffle 7″ wide. Double in half lengthwise and gather the double thickness to make full ruffles. Insert these in the seam when back and front are sewn together. Fill with fiberfill and stitch closed (see **Pillow Construction**).

Center line

BRIDAL WREATH QUILTED PILLOW

The Bridal Wreath appliqué quilt design is one of the loveliest—and one usually recommended for skilled quilt makers since applying all those slender vines, delicate leaves, and scalloped flowers takes a great deal of patience, especially if one is going to make enough squares to construct a full-size quilt. While not pretending that it equals lovely handwork, many quilt makers are happy that stenciling can be substituted to quickly make a quilt that will enhance a country bedroom.

Try this effect by making several accent pillows combining stenciling and quilting. Make them with pretty print ruffles and see how much fun they are.

Size: 14″ x 14″ excluding ruffle

MATERIALS

muslin, 100 percent cotton, 45″ wide—½ yard
print fabric, 100 percent cotton, 45″ wide—¾ yard
quilting fleece—17″ x 17″
stencil paints: rose, green, gold—small amounts of each
stencil film
quilting thread
fiberfill
stencil knife
washout pen or pencil
quilting needle
tracing paper

INSTRUCTIONS

Before proceeding with this project, prewash and iron muslin to avoid

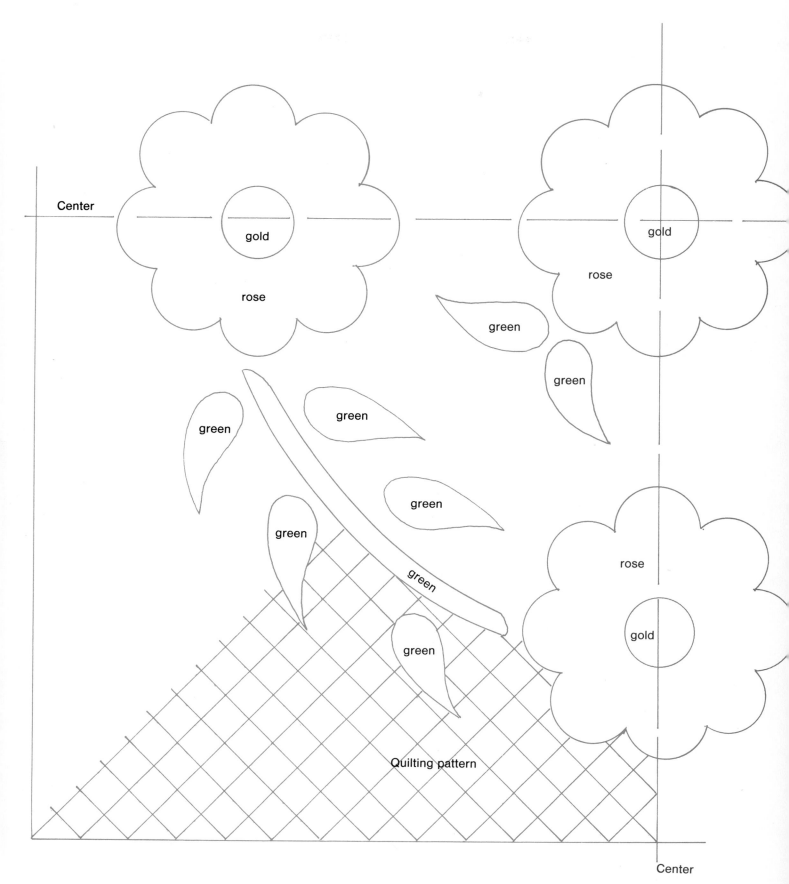

Center

gold

rose

gold

rose

green

green

green

green

green

green

green

green

green

rose

gold

Quilting pattern

Center

49

shrinkage problems.

This drawing shows one quarter of the Bridal Wreath design. To make a complete drawing, draw a 14" square on a piece of tracing paper. Fold the paper into quarters. Open it flat, place the fold lines over the slashed lines on the drawing, and trace the portion of design shown.

Move the tracing paper counterclockwise until the folds and lines match again and trace another quarter of the design. Repeat twice more to complete the design.

Make one 14" x 14" master stencil and cut out the leaves, vines, and flower centers from it. For the flower petals, a single flower cut from a smaller piece of stencil film will be sufficient since it can be moved and centered over the individual flower centers.

From the muslin cut two 16" x 16" squares. Use one for the pillow top, the other to back the quilting fleece.

Center the master stencil on one piece of muslin, and following the directions on the label, **stencil** the green and gold areas. Add the flowers, placing them as shown on the drawing. Set the colors according to the instructions on the label.

Mark the lines forming the diamond-pattern quilting design. The ones shown in this design are spaced ½" apart and form very small diamonds. If you prefer a more open pattern and less stitching, make the lines farther apart. Note how the quilting ends at the vine, leaving the center part unquilted.

Layer together the stenciled muslin, the quilting fleece, and the plain muslin square. Pin together and baste securely by running long stitches in rows back and forth across the piece.

Quilt around all the stenciled areas. If desired, a second row of stitches may be placed in the flowers, repeating the scallops about ¼" inside the colored area. Quilt also on the diamond-pattern lines.

Construct a pillow using the print fabric for ruffles and backing (see **Pillow Construction**).

If you have opted to make a full-size quilt, have fun! Your project will be something you enjoy both during its creation and later as part of your country bedroom.

PRESIDENT'S WREATH QUILTED PILLOW

Honoring an unnamed president, this wreath design is one of many circular floral appliqué quilt patterns. Since the quilt required a good deal of skill and a lot of work, most were prized—used only for special occasions—and thus many have survived to be handed down to succeeding generations.

Like most of the wreath designs, the original did not have the central bud motif, that large circular space instead being left to be embellished with an involved quilted design. Adding the motif and stenciling the color instead of appliquéing it makes the design a perfect one for a quick-to-make country accent. The tiny red floral print used for the cording and backing can also be used elsewhere in the room as a unifying element.

Size: 14" x 14"

MATERIALS

muslin, 100 percent cotton, 45" wide—
  ½ yard
print fabric, 100 percent cotton, 45"
  wide—⅝ yard
stencil paints: red, green
quilting fleece—17" x 17"
stencil film

quilting thread
fiberfill
cable cord—58"
washout pen or pencil
stencil knife
tracing paper
quilting needle

INSTRUCTIONS

The drawing shows a little more than one quarter of the President's Wreath design. To make a complete drawing, draw a 14" square on a piece of tracing paper. Fold the square into quarters. Open it flat, match the fold lines to the slashed lines on the drawing and trace the portion of design shown.

Refold the paper on the fold lines and trace the rest of the design through the paper, or move the open paper around three times and trace the balance of the design.

Make one master stencil and cut the leaves and vines from it. (It is possible to make a stencil of just one quarter of the design, looking much like the drawing, and to use it four times, thus saving a little time cutting the stencil, but it really is easier to place the larger one once and not worry about matching exactly with every move. The full-size stencil also makes centering the design on the muslin automatic.) Make another stencil for the flowers and buds, cutting out just one flower, one bud from the outer wreath, and one bud from the center group. Place these on the film as they are on the drawing; with the green in place it will be easy to move this stencil to do all the red.

From the muslin cut two 16" x 16" squares. Use one for the pillow top

and the other as the backing for the quilting fleece.

Center the master stencil on one piece of the muslin, and following the directions on the paint label, **stencil** all the green design. Add the flowers and buds, placing them as shown in the drawing. Set the color as directed by the manufacturer.

Mark the outline of the 14" x 14" square on the muslin. Use the outside edges of the master stencil for this if it was cut accurately. Using the drawing for the Bridal Wreath Pillow as a guide, mark the lines forming the diamond-pattern quilting design on the outside of the wreath, ending where the lines intersect color. (The quilting lines shown are spaced ½" apart and form very small diamonds. If you prefer a more open pattern and less stitching, make the lines farther apart.)

Layer together the stenciled muslin, the quilting fleece, and the plain muslin square. Pin together and baste securely with long stitches in rows about 2" apart.

Quilt around all stenciled areas. Work another row of stitches in each flower, following the outline and placing the row about ½" inside the outline. Quilt the background diamond pattern.

Remove any traces of the quilting lines in the diamond pattern. Use the print fabric for the pillow back. Cut bias strips to cover cable cord for insertion in the seam. It is shown here as a tailored piped pillow, but this design would be just as pretty with a country ruffle. (See **Pillow Construction** for details.)

red

green

red

green

green

red

green

green

red

red

53

BARGELLO BENCH PAD

The bench was not old, nor could it be considered a country piece, but it had to be used in the breakfast room no matter what its style. A Bargello-covered pad in a small overall design, worked in colors to match the rest of the room, was the first step in its conversion to the country look. Pillows, an old teddy bear, and a rag doll pulled it together and now no one even thinks about the bench's origins. It fits into the room and really belongs there.

Many Bargello patterns fit the country idiom, adding a pattern that combines well with the prints, checks, and stripes without clashing or overpowering their low-key effect. Bargello itself is a practical, long-wearing canvas embroidery that lends itself to upholstery and accessories like chair pads and pillows.

Small in scale and worked in just two colors, this pattern is particularly good in a country room. Color choice greatly affects its ability to fit into a decorating scheme. Most of the soft, old-looking country colors—slate blue, dark green, barn red, wood brown—

worked with off-white would be appropriate. Two dark colors also look wonderfully like old woven fabrics, my own favorite being the wine and blue of old coverlets with a tiny dash of white for the long stitches in the center of the diamonds.

MATERIALS

#17 mono canvas (see instructions for measuring below)
Persian yarn (see instructions for calculating below)
tapestry needle—#22
1″ foam pad cut to fit
backing fabric to fit
washout pen or pencil
heavy paper
masking tape
cable cord or ready-made cording

INSTRUCTIONS

Since every bench or chair seat will have different proportions, these are general instructions for making a seat pad to fit your own piece of furniture.

This seat pad was worked on a 17-mesh-to-the-inch yellow mono canvas. That at first may seem like a tedious project to undertake, but remember that most of the stitches are taken over four threads, some over six. The work goes fast and the resulting short stitches make a smooth surface that is not prone to snagging. If, however, this canvas is just too small a scale to fit your needs, choose another and adjust the yarn requirements to fit.

The canvas must be mono canvas—the threads merely cross, do not interlock. To determine the size needed, measure the seat and cut a paper pattern to fit. Add at least 3″ on all sides (if the seat is 12″ x 20″, cut the canvas at least 18" x 26"). If the shape is irregular, do not cut out that shape until after the finished embroidery is blocked.

Lay the paper pattern on the canvas and trace around it, placing the line 1" outside the edges of the pattern piece. Work the **Bargello** within these lines.

This Bargello pattern, worked with two strands of crewel wool on the #17 canvas, requires 8 yards of each of two colors to complete a 4" x 4" square (16 square inches).

To estimate the yardage needed for a particular project, figure the square inches to be embroidered, divide by 16, and then multiply by 8. For instance, if the piece is 10" x 16", the total square inches would be 160; 160 ÷ 16 = 10; 10 x 8 = 80. Thus 80 yards of each color are needed to make the 10" x 16" seat pad.

This estimate of yarn requirements is very accurate, with not a scrap wasted, so after finding the yardage needed, add an extra skein of each color to be sure you have enough to finish.

If you wish to change to a larger size canvas, begin by working a 4" swatch and carefully measure the yarn used. Use that quantity to figure requirements for the seat.

Bind the edges of the canvas with masking tape to prevent snagging and fraying. Center the design and begin work with color A to establish the diamond grid. You may work this pattern over the entire piece before filling in with color B, or you may add B as you progress. The latter method is more fun and is the way most canvas enthusiasts prefer to work.

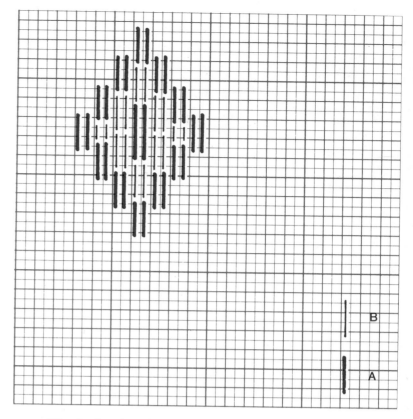

Block the finished piece (see page 118). Using the paper pattern, cut out the backing fabric, allowing ½" seam allowances on all sides. Cut the foam padding the same size as the backing. The extra inches make the foam fit snugly into the cover.

Make cording from bias strips of the backing fabric, or purchase ready-made cording to match or contrast. If ties are needed, cut them also from the backing fabric and finish them with a narrow machine-stitched hem.

Lay the cut backing fabric on the wrong side of the finished Bargello, and with a washout pen, draw the outline of the backing on the Bargello. Machine-stitch on the line to keep the work from fraying when cut. Trim the piece just outside the stitching line.

Baste the cording to the right side of the Bargello on the seam line. Pin the ties (if any) in place. Join the backing to the Bargello in a ½" seam, leaving most of the back side open for insertion of the foam. Trim the seam; turn. Insert the foam and close the opening.

BARGELLO COUNTRY FLOWERS PILLOW

Bargello is an old style of embroidery and as such can be found gracing European castles, early American mansions, country cottages, and every kind of home in between. Its geometric patterns adapt to any environment with a charm all their own. This little pillow enhances a country setting by offering a remembrance of flowers from a garden full of sunshine and cheer.

Size: 9½" x 9½"

MATERIALS

#14 mono canvas—14" x 14"
Persian yarn
  #611, dark green—35 yards
  #693, medium green—7 yards
  #861, rust—7 yards
  #932, medium rust—7 yards
  #406, pale peach—6 yards
  #756, cream—60 yards
muslin, 45" wide—¾ yard
tapestry needle—#24

fiberfill
masking tape

INSTRUCTIONS

Tape the edges of the canvas to prevent fraying and mark the canvas as in Chart #1 to divide it for four-way **Bargello:** Place the horizontal and vertical lines *A* and *B* first. Then, beginning at the center hole where these two cross, mark the two diagonal miter lines. Draw these lines accurately, placing a mark at the corner of each mesh so the canvas looks like Chart #2, which is an enlargement of the center portion of Chart #1. Note that these two miter lines are shown on the drawing of the Bargello pattern at the top left and the bottom right. They extend from the center to the borders, but they will not be apparent under the stitches.

Work the **Bargello stitches** with two strands of the Persian yarn. Begin working at the top of Segment One by placing the dark green stitches marked *1, 2,* and *3.* Note that stitch direction changes at the miter lines. To keep the miter lines straight, it is necessary sometimes to change the stitch length along these lines, and the chart shows this adjustment.

Work all of Segment One, following the chart for color placement and for any changes in stitch length. Use basic good Bargello technique and stay within the miter lines.

Turn the canvas and work the adjacent segment, placing the stitches as in the completed one. Finish all four two-part sections.

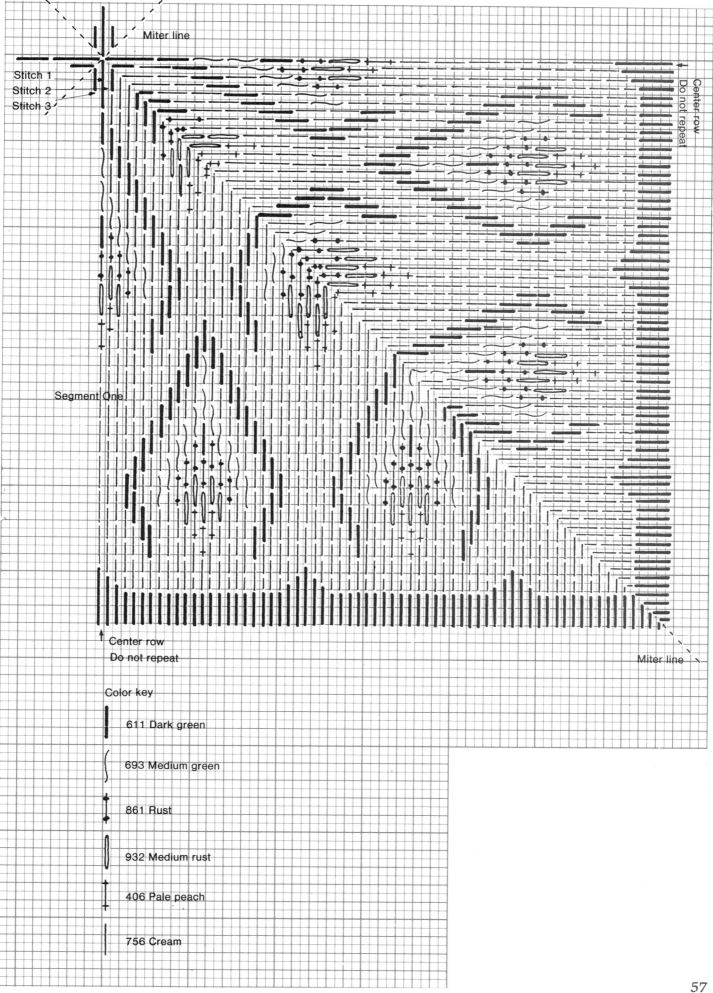

Miter line

Stitch 1
Stitch 2
Stitch 3

Center row
Do not repeat

Segment One

Center row
Do not repeat

Miter line

Color key

611 Dark green

693 Medium green

861 Rust

932 Medium rust

406 Pale peach

756 Cream

Chart #1

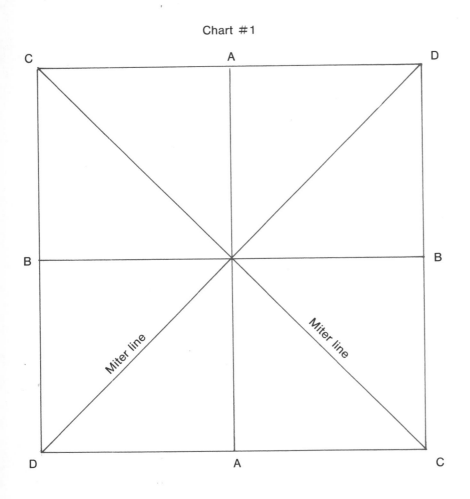

Block as described on page 118.

Cut two 6″-wide strips of muslin across the full width of the fabric. Join them in seams to make a continuous strip. Fold this in half lengthwise and gather the doubled fabric on the cut edge to make a ruffle that fits the outside edge of the pillow top.

Trim away the unworked canvas borders of the Bargello, leaving a ½″ seam allowance. Use the trimmed Bargello as a pattern to cut muslin for the pillow back.

Construct the pillow, inserting the ruffle in the seam. Stuff with fiberfill and stitch closed. (See **Pillow Construction** for details.)

This diagram represents a canvas with the four guidelines marked for four-way Bargello. Lines *A* and *B* divide the canvas into four quarters. Lines *C* and *D* are the miter lines.

This enlarged detail of the center portion of a marked canvas shows the dividing lines as dots as they will appear on the canvas. Note the way lines *C* and *D* move out from the center mesh on the true diagonal. It is important these lines be drawn accurately.

Chart #2

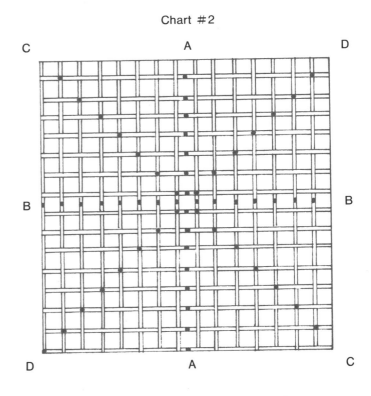

SWAN WEATHERVANE PICTURE

Until recently old American weathervanes formed a category of antique collectibles that was largely ignored, and examples could be bought for reasonable prices. A grouping of both metal and wooden ones makes an interesting display, for the artistry in most weathervanes is truly beautiful. Even crudely cut shapes often have spectacular lines, and the weathered finishes of both materials are lovely.

But collectors did discover the wonderful old pieces and prices have skyrocketed, so most of us will have to enjoy their unique beauty in museums or photographs. The graceful swan that is the center of both this design and the hooked rug on page 87 is one weathervane that has found a home in a museum.

Colors, basic layout, and design of the needlepoint picture and the hooked rug are almost the same, making them an attractive pair of accents. The colors chosen are based on a "country collection" of all-cotton fabrics which were cut into strips for hooking the rug. It was fairly easy to

match yarn for the needlepoint with the dusty colors of the cotton. The popularity of the country theme in decorating has made it possible to obtain these soft colors easily.

Size: 9½″ x 16″

MATERIALS

#14 mono canvas—16″ x 22″
Persian yarn
  #263, white—20 yards
  #220, black—40 yards
  #454, tan—15 yards
  #932, light rose—10 yards
  #930, medium rose—12 yards
  #701, gold—10 yards
  #342, purple—12 yards
  #613, light green—10 yards
  #620, medium green—12 yards
  #661, dark green—12 yards
  #502, blue—60 yards
  #571, navy—22 yards
tapestry needle—#20 or #22
masking tape
fabric marking pen or pencil
framing materials

INSTRUCTIONS

Following the instructions on page 114 for making a complete drawing from divided drawings, make a tracing of the design. Use a heavy line so the drawing can be seen through the canvas.

Bind the edges of the canvas with masking tape to prevent fraying. Center the canvas over the drawing, and using a permanent-ink pen, trace the design onto the canvas. Be careful to trace the straight lines along a thread of the canvas and to draw the diagonals of the border on the true bias line of the canvas.

It is best to work as much as possible of the piece using the **basket weave stitch.** If this is a problem on the irregularly shaped spaces, outline them first with **continental stitch** in the color indicated and then fill in with the basket weave stitch.

The upper right corner of the blue field is a good place to begin stitching. Work the background until it meets the pink flower. Work the flower and the leaves, then continue with the background until you get to the swan. Working in this manner prevents a great deal of canvas distortion and divides the background area into lots of small areas to be worked between the more interesting design areas.

Finish the central panel and then begin the border, leaving the narrow black outside edge until last. In the border, stitch the dividing lines between the colored triangles with black yarn. Also make the vines and the leaf outlines black.

When the needlepoint is complete, block it (see page 118) and frame it in a simple frame.

Reduced versions of the swan design can be used for a number of embroidery projects. Find a quick-print shop that has a copy machine that reduces and make several smaller versions of the swan. A row of swans embroidered with **outline stitch** on one of the new lace-trimmed muslin bands would embellish a set of towels. Or you could embroider the swans directly onto other accessories. You'll find that there are lots of uses for small motifs like this one.

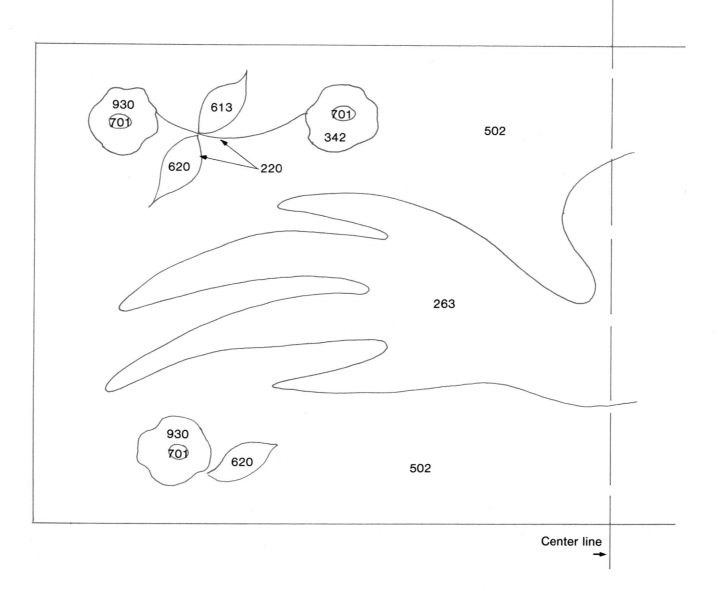

Center line

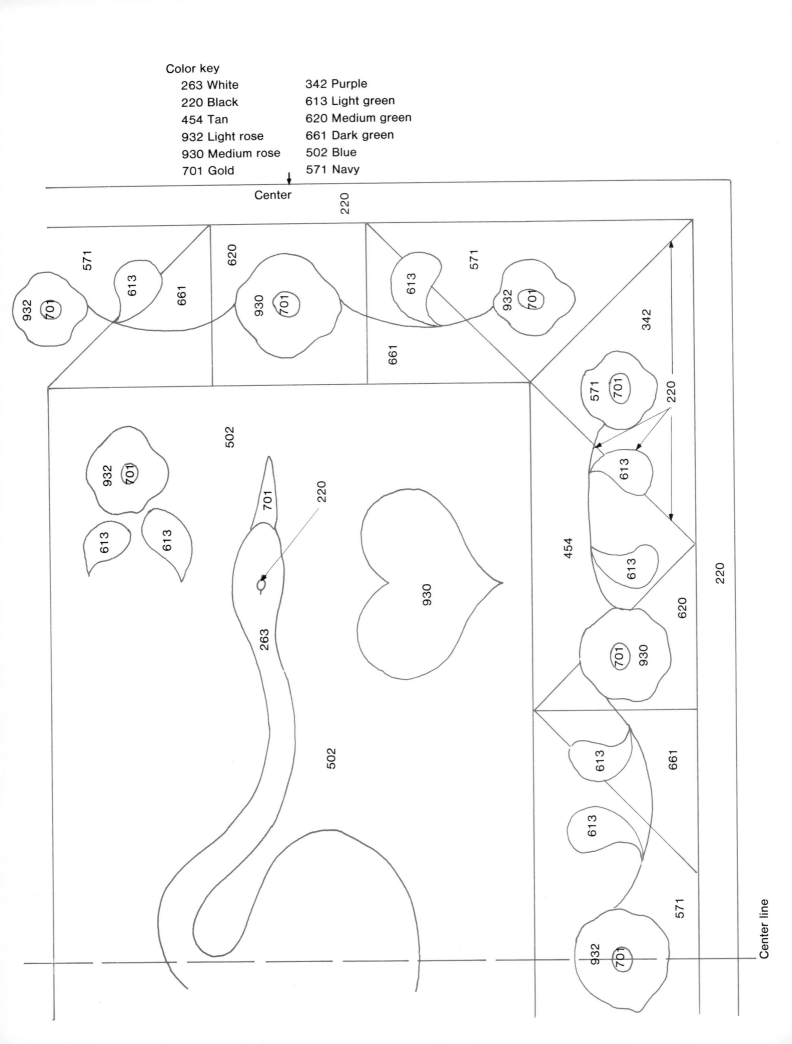

Color key
263 White   342 Purple
220 Black   613 Light green
454 Tan   620 Medium green
932 Light rose   661 Dark green
930 Medium rose   502 Blue
701 Gold   571 Navy

NEEDLEPOINT WELCOME

Crayon-bright country colors and a number of patterns combine to make a cheerful "Welcome." Worked on a fine canvas with cotton embroidery floss, this is a refreshing change from wool yarn and larger mesh. A touch of stenciling brightens the mat and adds a personal touch.

The finished picture is small but bright. To enlarge it, work on larger mesh canvas and change to wool yarn. Or use the design on linen for a cross stitch picture. This would result in a change in general appearance and would take much less time, as the green background and all the ecru areas could be left unworked.
Size: 5¼" x 6¾"

MATERIALS

#18 canvas—9½" x 10½"
DMC embroidery floss
   white—2 skeins
   #934, dark green—3 skeins
   #469, medium green—1 skein
   #472, light green—1 skein
   #347, red—2 skeins
   ecru—3 skeins
   #336, colonial blue—2 skeins
   #740, orange—1 skein
   #928, gray—1 skein
   #761, rose—1 skein
   black—several inches for eye
tracing paper
masking tape
tapestry needle—#26
mat
stencil brush
stencil film
stencil paint: ecru—small amount
stencil knife
framing materials

INSTRUCTIONS

Bind the canvas edges with masking tape to prevent fraying. Use the full six strands of floss for the needlepoint. Before threading the needle, separate the strands to remove the twist, then put them back together. This makes the thread easier to use, and it will cover the canvas better. If, when working some of the dark colors, the area seems sparsely covered, either add one or two more strands of thread or tint the canvas before working those areas. If extra thread is used, increase the quantity called for in the materials list.

Work as much of the picture as possible in the **basket weave stitch,** beginning at the upper right corner and working downward. Use white for the goose, dark green for the floral background, and the other colors as noted on the chart.

Block the completed needlepoint (see page 118). Frame as shown in a primitive frame with a wide mat accented with an ecru stencil.

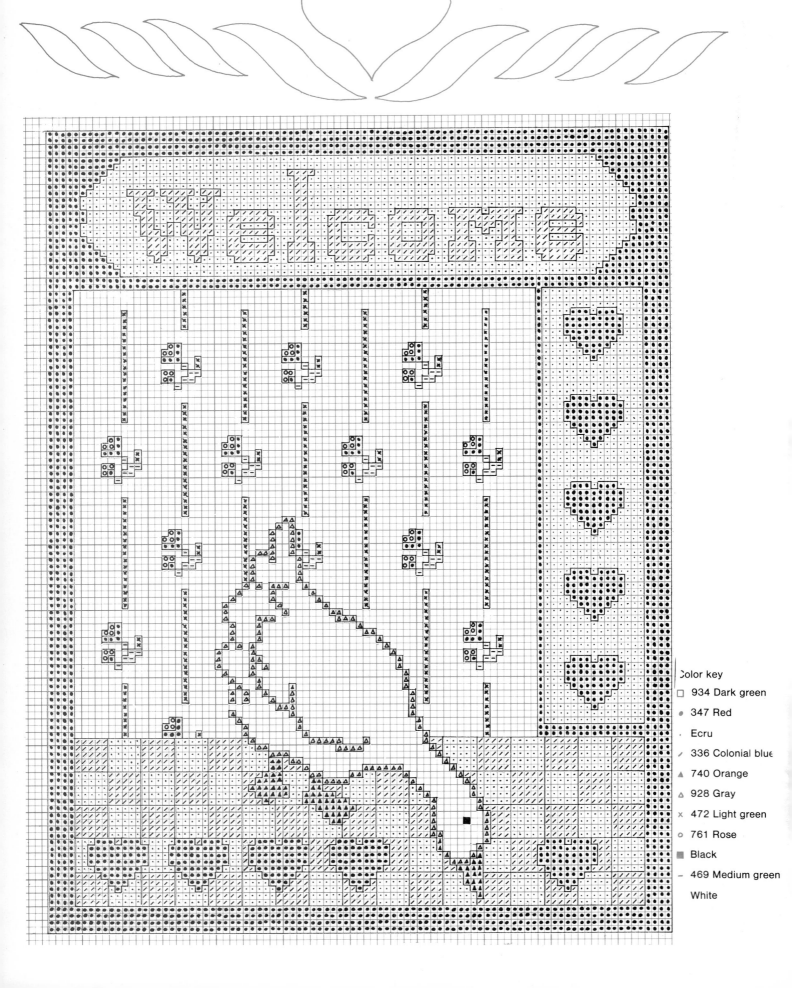

Color key

☐ 934 Dark green

● 347 Red

· Ecru

╱ 336 Colonial blue

▲ 740 Orange

△ 928 Gray

✕ 472 Light green

○ 761 Rose

■ Black

– 469 Medium green

White

Left:
Ohio Star
Quilted Pillow
(p. 31); Angel
Gabriel Quilted
Pillow (p. 28);
Candlewick
Fantasy Pillow
(p. 85); Winged
Gabriel Hooked
Rug (p. 94)

Right:
Autumn Leaves
Patchwork
Hanging (p. 34);
Country Dolls
(p. 10)

Candlewick
Christmas
Wreath (p. 74)

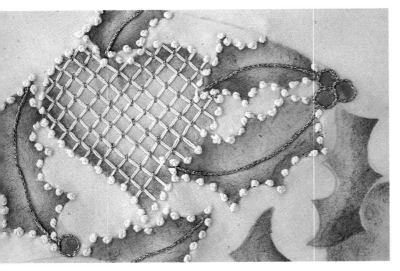

Details: Bargello Bench Pad (p. 54); Candlewick Fantasy Pillow (p. 85); Candlewick Christmas Wreath (p. 74); Winged Gabriel Hooked Rug and Stenciled Floorcloth (p. 94); Christmas Heart Ornament (p. 71); Doll Quilt (p. 21); Miniature Cross Stitch Picture (p. 101)

COUNTRY FLOWERS PILLOW

Ruffles seem to be an integral part of the country mood, often imbuing a piece with the naive quality that makes it part of this popular theme. A double chintz ruffle picking up the navy background color of this little needlepoint pillow adds country charm to a technique that is usually more formal. The simple design, worked in just three shades of pink and three of green, also contributes to the mood.

Other background colors that would suit this design are dark brown, black, beige, or off-white. With brown or beige, a change of flower colors from the pink tones to salmon or yellow would be lovely.

Size: 11¾″ x 11¾″

Color key

500 Navy
   (background)
845 Red
850 Medium red
860 Pink
692 Deep green
693 Medium green
694 Pale green

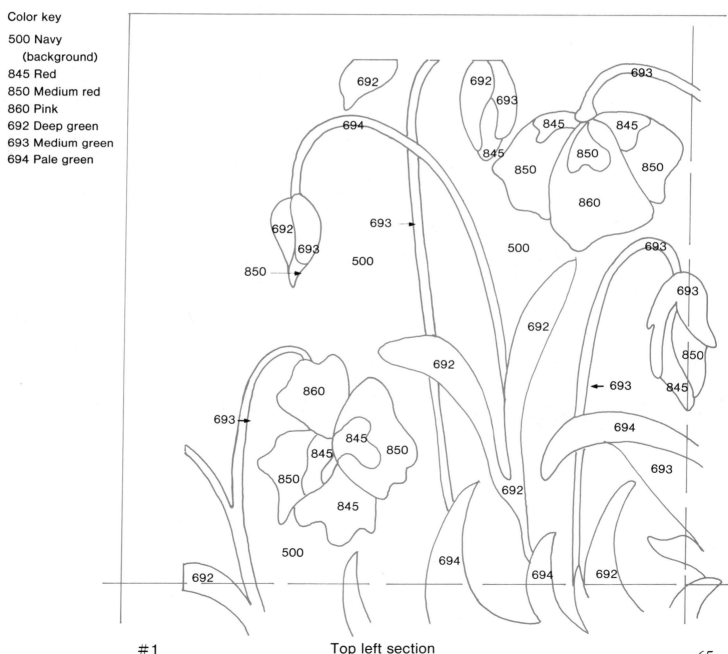

#1   Top left section

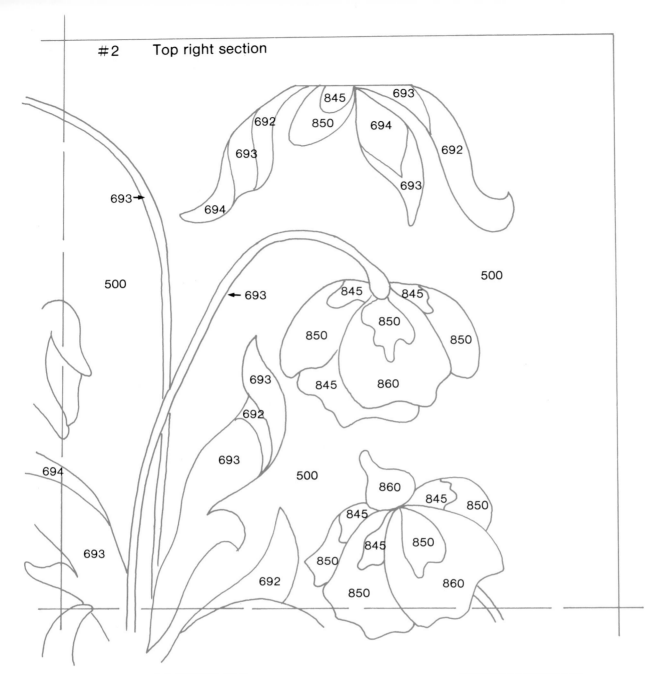

MATERIALS

#14 mono canvas—18″ x 18″
Persian yarn
   #500, navy (background)—115 yards
   #845, red—10 yards
   #850, medium red—15 yards
   #860, pink—10 yards
   #692, deep green—20 yards
   #693, medium green—25 yards
   #694, pale green—15 yards
tapestry needle—#22
chintz—1 yard
fiberfill
fabric marking pen
masking tape

INSTRUCTIONS

Following the instructions on page 114, make a complete tracing of the floral design. Make the drawing lines heavy so they can be traced through the needlepoint canvas.

Bind the edges of the canvas with masking tape to prevent fraying. Center the canvas over the drawing, and with a fine-point permanent marker, trace the design onto the canvas.

As you work the design, use the **basket weave stitch** as much as possible to prevent distortion of the canvas. Sometimes with small irregular shapes

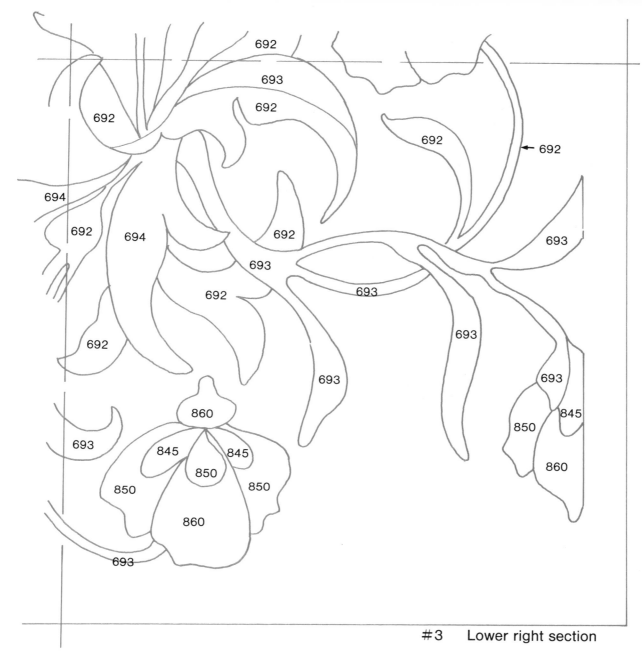

692

693

692

692

692

694

692 694

692

693

692

693

693

692

693

693

693

693

860

845 845

850

850 850

693

860

845

850

860

693

#3   Lower right section

it is helpful to outline the shape with **continental stitch** and then fill in with the basket weave.

Start working the background at the upper right corner to establish the alternating-row pattern of basket weave and maintain that sequence throughout the piece.

Complete the needlepoint, working in the colors noted on the four charts. Block the needlepoint (see page 118) and construct the pillow, using the chintz for the backing and a 2″ double ruffle (see **Pillow Construction**). Fill with fiberfill and close the opening.

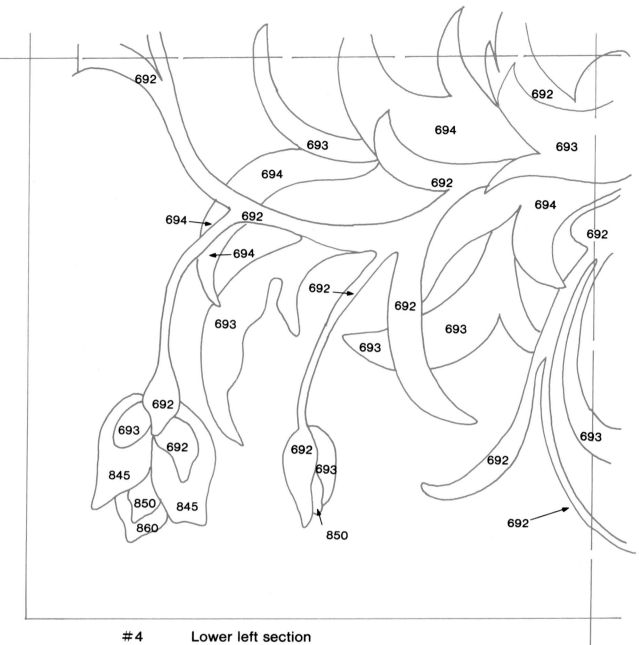

#4   Lower left section

HERITAGE CANDLEWICK PILLOW

The simple elegance of cotton yarn, homey muslin, familiar stitches, an off-white color scheme, and a romantic ruffle combine to make candlewick an embroidery with a natural country mood that has been used in home furnishing throughout our history. Try a pillow first, then branch out into curtains or a coverlet to make traditional use of this heritage country look.
Size: 14″ x 14″ excluding ruffle

MATERIALS

muslin, 45″ wide—1 yard
candlewick yarn—60 yards
chenille needle—#20
fiberfill
hoop
transfer pencil
tracing paper

INSTRUCTIONS

The drawing shows one half of the design. To make a complete drawing, make a 14″ square on tracing paper. Fold it in half. Open flat and place the fold line over the slashed line on the drawing, centering the drawing in the square. Trace the half design shown. Fold the paper again and trace the other section through the paper. The individual stitches are drawn, but don't bother to copy all of these. Just draw outlines, leaving out the short lines between the French knots, and also the seeding and trellis couching lines.

Go over the drawing with a transfer pencil. With a hot iron, transfer the design to a 16″ square of muslin.

Since the stitches of candlewick are large and the yarn bulky, it is best to work with the piece stretched in a hoop. Use three strands of candlewick yarn for the **French knots** and two strands for the **trellis couching** and **seeding** stitches.

The individual French knots are drawn on the lines that they form. Try spacing yours about the same distance apart. With the three strands of yarn the knots will probably be large enough to just touch each other and form a continuous line. If they seem too far apart, place them a little bit closer together. It may take more knots than drawn to fill in the small circles.

Use the drawing as a guide for the angle at which to slant the laid threads of the trellis couching and as an idea for spacing the seeding stitches.

When the embroidery is completed, wash it to remove the transfer lines. Do not wring. Roll it in a towel and press to remove excess water. Place the embroidery wrong side up over a thick towel and iron dry. Apply the iron to the wrong side only.

Use the remainder of the muslin to cut a 15″ square for the pillow back. To make the full double ruffle, cut three strips 5½″ wide across the full width of the muslin. Join the strips into a continuous piece. Fold it in half

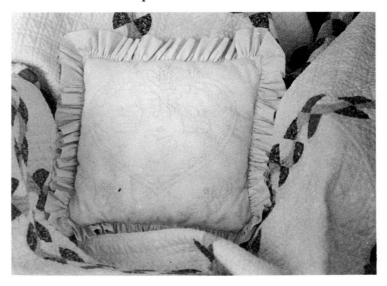

lengthwise and gather the raw edges to fit the 14″ square. Pin the ruffle to the embroidered top. Seam the top to the back, leaving an opening for turning. Trim the seam, turn, and stuff with fiberfill. Close the opening (see **Pillow Construction**).

B

B

B

B

B

B

B

A

A

B

C

B

B

B

B

Stitches
A Trellis couching
B Seeding
C French knots

CHRISTMAS HEART ORNAMENTS

Decorating for Christmas is fun no matter what the style of the home, but in a country house there is a special kind of nostalgia that makes everything more wonderful. In some magic way the slightly worn old toys, baskets, ruffles, lace, and interesting keepsakes combine with the gingerbread and holly scents of the season for pure magic.

A country-style tree can be anything from an unornamented evergreen to one covered completely with a collection of toys or other fanciful decorations. To add a little of that special magic, this set of muslin ornaments is planned to be this year's addition. They may be finished with the embroidery on one side only, or both back and front may be embellished. Consider also using the backs for a special message—the name of the maker, the name of the person to whom they are given, the date, or "Merry Christmas." Use your own script for this and embroider with **back stitch** in yarn, embroidery floss, or metallic thread.
Size: 3″ x 3½″

MATERIALS

muslin—¼ yard
cotton lace, 1″ wide—4 yards
cotton candlewick yarn (4 ply)—20 yards
gold metallic thread—11 yards
gold sewing thread
fiberfill
embroidery hoop
chenille needle or large crewel needle
heavy tracing paper
transfer pencil
ribbon, ⅛″ wide, ecru—1½ yards

INSTRUCTIONS

Trace the ornament designs onto heavy tracing paper. Go over the outlines with a transfer pencil and iron them onto the muslin, taking care to place the ornaments far enough apart to allow for a ½″ seam outside the stitching lines of each one. Do not cut out the individual hearts. The larger piece of fabric is easier to handle and fits into an embroidery hoop if left intact.

Using two ply of the candlewick yarn and a single strand of the metallic

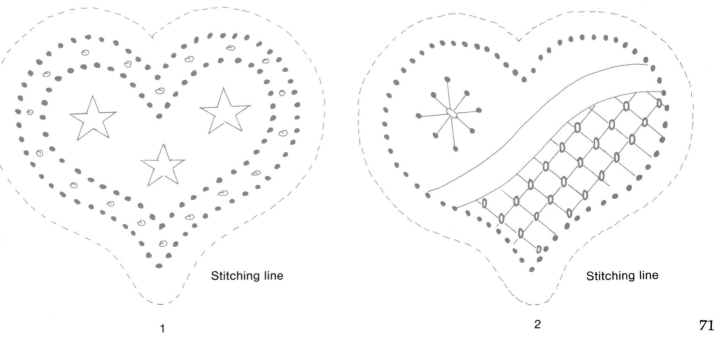

Stitching line

Stitching line

1

2

thread where each is indicated, embroider the hearts following the notes below.

Heart #1 Make a **French knot** with candlewick yarn on each black dot. With metallic thread make a French knot on each larger open circle. Form stars with metallic thread, laying the thread as for **couching** and fastening it at the points with gold sewing thread.

Heart #2 Use **trellis couching** for the lower section, laying the candlewick yarn and fastening it at the intersections with a short gold **straight stitch**. Work parallel curved lines in **running stitch** with candlewick yarn. **Whip** the running stitch with metallic thread. Make the star with **French knots on a long thread,** using the candlewick yarn. Add a short straight stitch over the center. Finish with French knots made with candlewick yarn around the outline of the heart.

Heart #3 Use candlewick yarn to make the **French knots** outlining the

holly leaves and the heart itself. The veins of the leaves should be **running stitch** of candlewick yarn **whipped** with the metallic thread. Form the berries with the gold metallic thread **couched** in place with gold sewing thread. The larger open circles on the chart indicate French knots in the gold metallic thread.

Heart #4 With candlewick yarn, make two rows of **French knots** around the edge of the heart as shown by the black dots. Use **trellis couching** for the center, laying the candlewick yarn and fastening it at the intersections with short upright **straight stitches.**

Heart #5 Use candlewick yarn for **French knots** on all black dots on the drawing. Work the two curved solid lines in **running stitch** with the candlewick yarn, **whipping** it with the gold metallic thread.

Heart #6 Make the three stars as directed for Heart #2. Place **French**

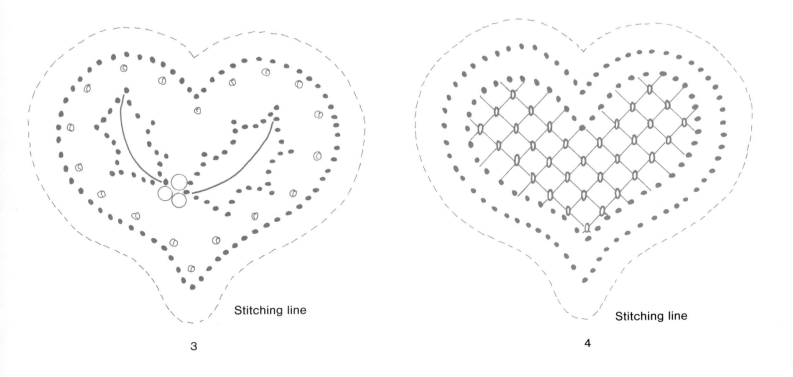

Stitching line

Stitching line

3

4

knots in candlewick yarn on all black dots. Work the two curved lines in **whipped running stitch** as in Heart #5.

Press the completed embroidery as necessary. Do not cut out the hearts.

Place the piece of fabric with the embroidered ornaments on another piece of muslin with right sides together. Pin or baste together. Using each outside row of French knots as a guide, stitch the two layers together on a line ¼″ outside the French knots, leaving an opening on each heart for stuffing.

Now cut the hearts apart, trimming the seams to ¼″. Turn the hearts right side out. Fill lightly with fiberfill, and close the opening. Whip 24″ of gathered lace to the edges of each heart, joining the ends of the lace at the top center where it is least apparent.

Cut the ribbon into six 9″ pieces and attach each piece in a loop at the top back of an ornament.

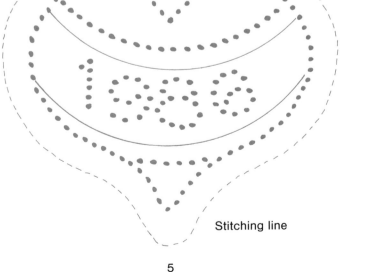

Stitching line

5

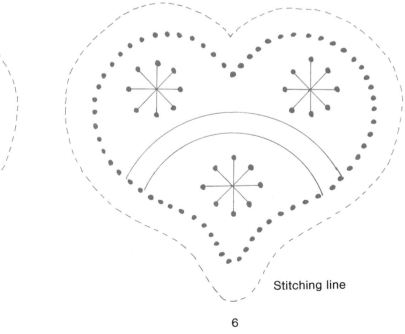

Stitching line

6

CANDLEWICK CHRISTMAS WREATH

A country Christmas! Even the words evoke special memories. Remembrances of simpler times, happy family traditions, holiday fragrances, and treasured keepsakes combine to make us think a true country celebration—even in the city—would be pure magic. Nostalgia does wonderful things for our rushed mundane days.

In most families holiday preparation is a ritual of traditions, and in most the love of making both gifts and decorations brings a special delight to the festivities. Many find additional joy in making a new keepsake each year to add to a growing collection. No collector ever finishes collecting!

To add to a country collection, a muslin and candlewick wreath brings a homespun look to complement pine boughs and baskets. This is a project to begin as soon as the first frost appears so it will be ready when the time comes to unpack ornaments and trimmings. Start early, not because there is a lot of time involved in making the wreath, but because it's nice to have things like this ready early so there's plenty of time for last-minute activities.

The wreath photographed here is made in the favored traditional off-white color scheme of candlewicking. There's a lot of texture in this embroidery, making it an interesting technique for Christmas decoration. The big muslin bow is cut from the same fabric used for the background; it looks lavish but is very inexpensive and will need only to be pressed next year.

Two suggestions for variations of the wreath feature stenciling and some gold embroidery accents. These add color and glitter while retaining the country look.

A detail of one alternative is shown in the color pages. There the design is stenciled in green and red with candlewick-yarn French knots outlining all the colored areas. Trellis couching is used over the red hearts. The laid threads are cotton candlewick yarn; the tie-down threads are metallic gold. This same gold is couched with a single strand of matching embroidery floss to outline the berries and veins in the leaves. Candlewick yarn could be substituted for the gold in all three places, creating yet another look.

In the second variation the stenciling is the same, but all the embroidery is couched gold to make a really sparkling wreath. One-inch-wide cotton Cluny lace was added to the ruffle on this sample.

Size: 16" diameter excluding ruffle

Section #1

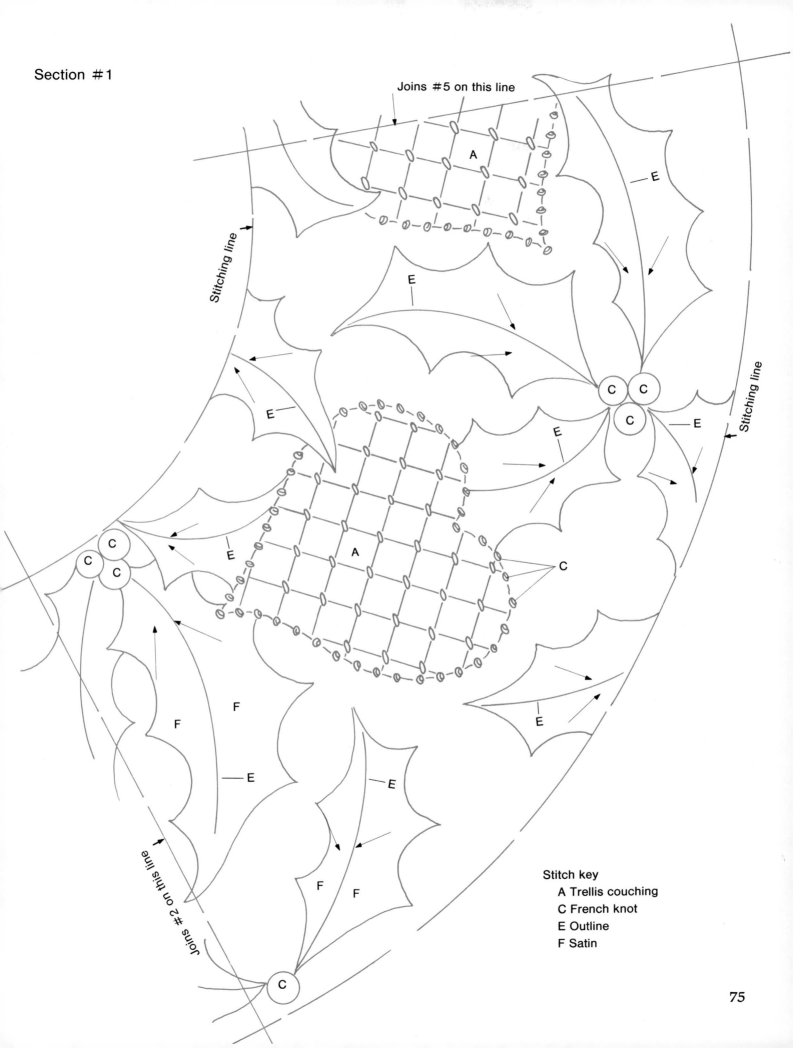

Joins #5 on this line

Stitching line

Stitching line

Joins #2 on this line

A

E

E

E

E

E

E

E

E

E

E

E

C

C

C

C

C

C

C

A

F

F

F

F

C

Stitch key
A Trellis couching
C French knot
E Outline
F Satin

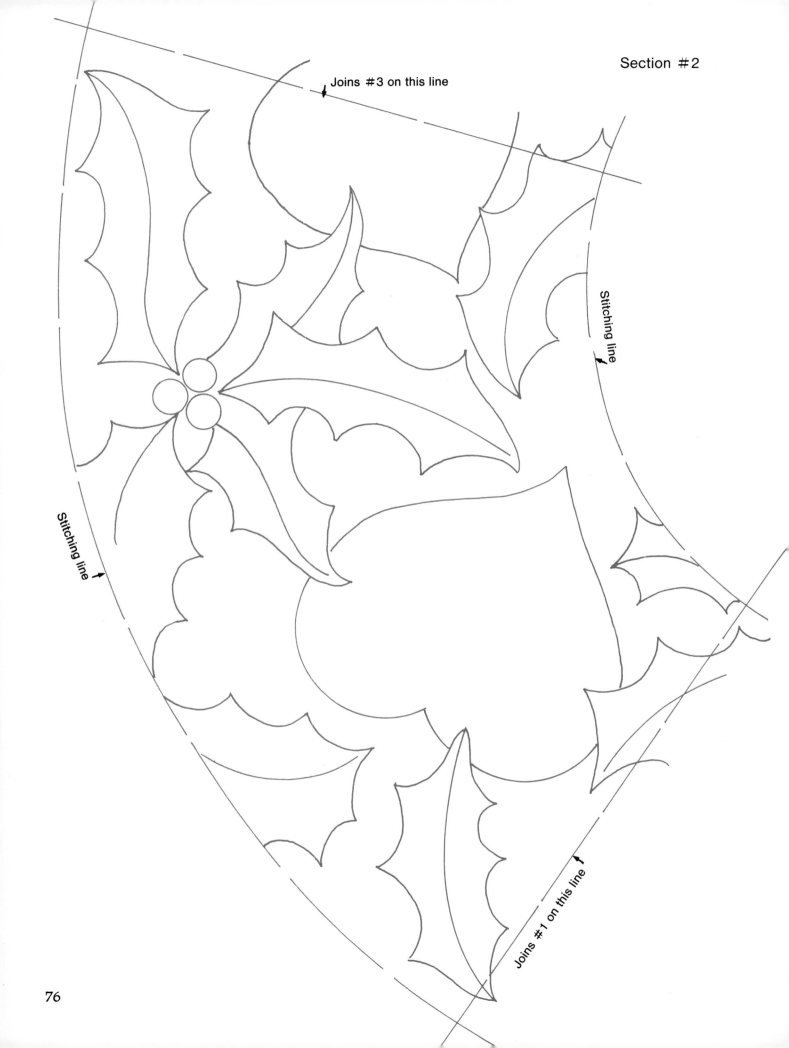

Joins #3 on this line

Stitching line

Stitching line

Joins #1 on this line

Section #3

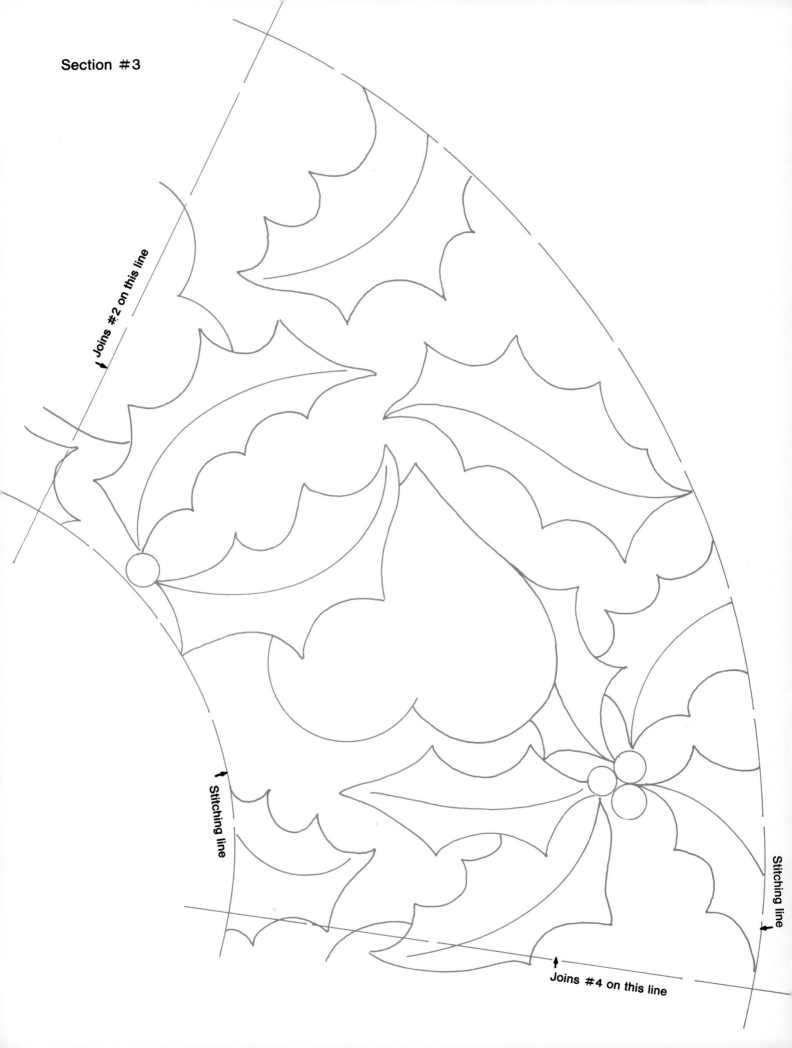

Joins #2 on this line

Stitching line

Stitching line

Joins #4 on this line

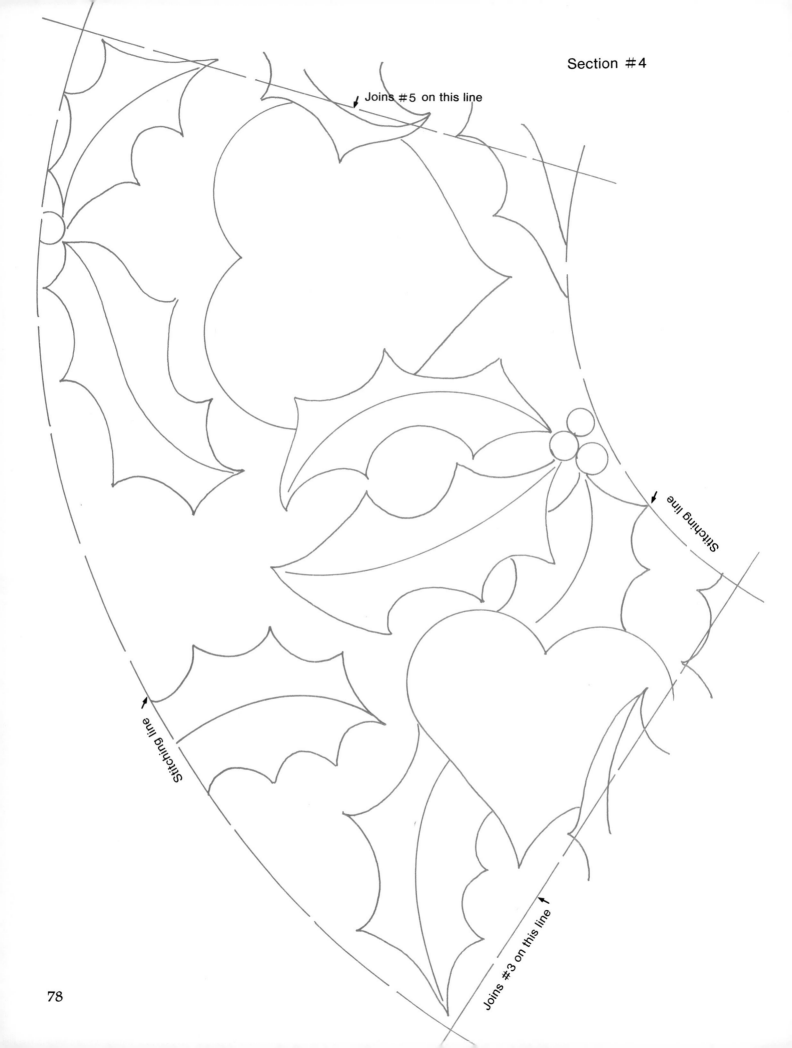

Joins #5 on this line

Stitching line

Stitching line

Joins #3 on this line

Section #5

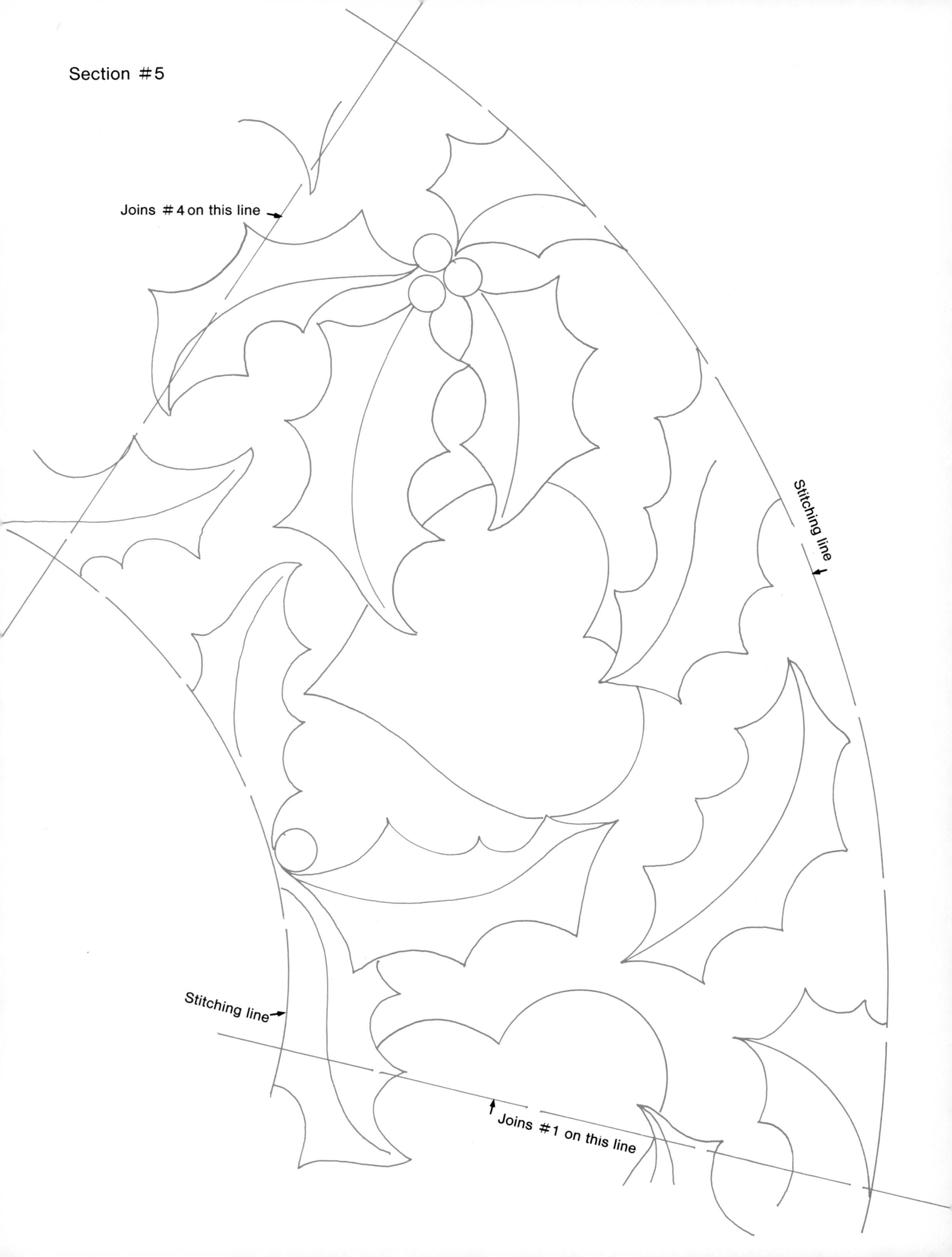

Joins #4 on this line →

Stitching line ↓

Stitching line →

↑ Joins #1 on this line

MATERIALS

muslin, 45″ wide—1¼ yards
candlewick yarn—75 yards
spray adhesive or craft glue
foamcore board—17″ x 17″
fiberfill
craft knife
tracing paper
transfer pencil
embroidery hoop or frame
chenille needle
desk stapler and staples for tacking

INSTRUCTIONS

This large design has been divided into five sections. The small drawing illustrates how the pieces fit together to form a circle. Each segment is numbered on the large drawings and on the small sketch. In addition, a notation on the end of each segment indicates which segment it joins.

Copy all five sections to form the complete pattern on a large sheet of tracing paper. Match the slashed lines of one to those of the next one. A small amount of design overlaps to help with placement.

Note that on Section 1 the French knots outlining the hearts and the grid of the trellis couching are shown. Don't try to copy these. Using the small lines between the French knots as a guide, make the drawing look like the other four. Trace the stitching lines on all segments.

From the muslin cut three strips 6″ wide across the 45″ width of the fabric. Set these aside for the ruffle. Fold the remaining piece of muslin in half on the bias and cut two 3″-wide bias strips across the full length of the bias fold. These are for the bow.

Use the remaining fabric to cut one 24″ square and two 19″ squares. Piece one or both of the smaller ones if necessary.

Go over the drawing of the wreath with a transfer pencil and apply it to the 24″ square of muslin. (Twenty-four inches is a little larger than necessary, but makes working in the hoop easier.) Leave the fabric square for now; do not trim it.

Place the 24″ muslin square in a hoop or frame. Embroider, using the drawing of Section 1 as the guide for placement of stitches. On the drawing the French knots are smaller than yours will be, but their placement is accurate. They should form a solid but uncrowded line. You may need to work yours slightly closer or with a little more space between them to make a nice line.

Use four strands of the candlewick yarn for the French knots and outline stitch, two for trellis couching, and a single strand for the satin stitch.

To work a heart, lay the threads for the **trellis couching,** tie them down with short upright stitches, then work the outline of **French knots.** Berries should be a cluster of approximately seven French knots. The holly leaves are **satin stitch** worked to slant toward the base of the leaves. Arrows on the drawing of Section 1 show the direction of the slant of these stitches. Leave a very narrow space on the vein line of each leaf. Work the **outline stitch** vein in that space.

With the sewing machine, run a row of reinforcement stitching along both stitching lines. Wash the completed embroidery to remove any traces of the transfer pencil; do not wring it. Lift the material out of the water, roll it in a towel, and press to remove most of the water. Put a heavy towel on the ironing board and place the embroidery on the towel, wrong side up. Iron dry, taking care not to scorch the fabric.

Trim the outside of the embroidered piece ½″ outside the stitching line. Cut a 4″ circle from the middle of the inner circle. Slash the remaining portion of that inner circle in pie-shaped wedges to the stitching line, taking care not to clip the stitches. The slashes should be about 1″ apart where they meet the stitching line.

Use the trimmed wreath piece as a pattern to cut two more circles from the two 19″ squares of muslin. Cut away enough of the center of one of the circles to leave a 3½″-wide wreath piece to use as a facing.

Construct the ruffle by joining the three 6″-wide strips into a continuous piece. Fold in half lengthwise. Pin the edges together and run two rows of machine gathering along the raw edge. Pull up the gathers to fit the outside circumference of the circle. Stitch the ruffle to the right side of the embroidery, raw edges together. Stitch the 3½″ facing to the wreath along the outside edge.

Cut a 16″-diameter circle from the foamcore board. This is smaller than the embroidery, but it is correct. Make an opening in the center of the circle the same as that of the embroidery (8″). This material cuts easily with a craft knife.

Apply glue to a 1″-wide border around the inner opening of the foamcore circle. Place the fabric wreath on a flat surface with the wrong side facing up. Lay the foam foundation on top, glue-coated side facing up, matching the center openings. Pull the slashed pieces of muslin to the top and fasten by pressing them into the glue. Pull tightly enough so that the stitching line will not be visible on the right side. If the fabric won't lie flat along the curve, slash again to the stitching line. Allow to dry.

Turn the wreath over. Working carefully, turn the facing so it fits over the foamcore for about one quarter of

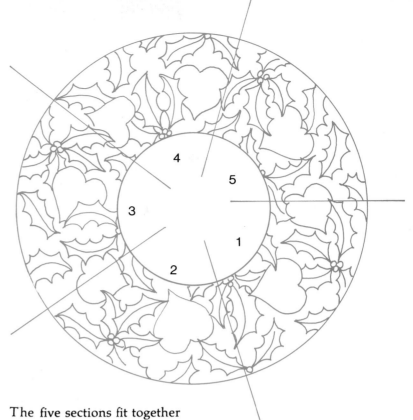

The five sections fit together to make a full circle.

the circle. You will need to make clips in the facing in order to get it over the foamcore without breaking it. Stuff the embroidered side of the fitted section with fiberfill, carefully working it in. Use a pencil or other tool to push it close to the edges on both sides. As you fill an area, turn back more of the facing and gradually work around the wreath. Stuff firmly to support the embroidery.

Pull the facing tightly to the back and check to make sure the stuffing is even. Staple the facing in place. Make a small loop of the candlewick yarn and attach it to the top of the wreath with several staples.

Turn under the raw edges of the remaining muslin circle and glue or staple it to the back of the wreath to cover the raw edges.

Spray the two bias muslin strips with starch and iron dry. This and the bias cut prevent fraying. Make a large bow and attach it to one side as shown in the photograph.

COLONIAL EAGLE CANDLEWICK PILLOW

Patriotic and political symbols have always been important in American folk art and embroidery. The eagle has been one of the most prominent, probably both because it speaks of patriotism in ways we all understand and also simply because it is such a beautiful form. Worked in the monochromatic color scheme and textured stitches of candlewick, its graphic form is as appealing today as it was two hundred years ago.
Size: 14″ x 14″

MATERIALS

muslin, 45″ wide—¾ yard
candlewick yarn—50 yards
cotton cable cord—3¼ yards
fiberfill
chenille needle—#20
embroidery hoop
tracing paper
transfer pencil

INSTRUCTIONS

To combine the eagle and border designs into one, begin by drawing a 14″ square on tracing paper. Draw a 10″ square inside the 14″ one, centering it 2″ in from the edges. Fold the paper in quarters, aligning the corners of the squares. Then open the paper flat and place it over the drawing of the eagle, matching the folds of the paper to the center lines. Trace the eagle.

Move the tracing paper to the drawing of the border. Match the fold lines of the paper and the center lines of the drawing, and trace the star and small circles onto the lower left quarter of the paper. The lines at the ends of the circles are guidelines only. These should fall on the outlines of the 10″ square.

Fold the paper in half vertically and trace the lower right section of the border through the paper.

The stars must be slightly repositioned in the two upper corners. Using the placement of the lower stars as a guide, trace the two upper ones on the corners of the 10″ square so that the horizontal line that can be drawn across the top of points #1 and #2 lies on the horizontal line which is the top of the 10″ square. Check to make certain the point of #1 (on the left) or that of #2 (on the right) extends beyond the vertical line the same distance as the corresponding point of the star in the lower corner. Use the border drawing to trace the remaining small circles, noting that the ones on the side borders are not perfectly centered, to allow for the assymmetrical shape of the stars.

From the muslin cut one 18″

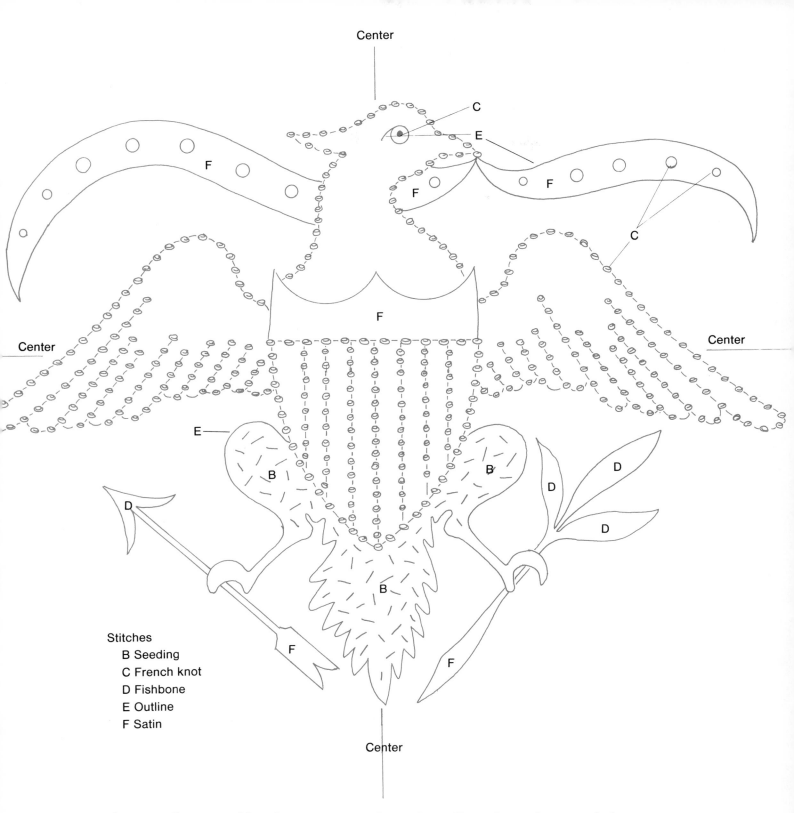

Center

C

E

F

F

F

C

Center

Center

F

E

B

B

D

D

D

D

E

B

Stitches
B Seeding
C French knot
D Fishbone
E Outline
F Satin

F

F

B

F

Center

square and one 15″ square. Use the balance to cut a 3″-wide strip 56″ long (piece if necessary). Also cut on the true bias enough 1″-wide strips to cover the 3¼ yards of cable cord.

Go over the drawing with a transfer pencil. With a hot iron, transfer it to the 18″ square of muslin. Since the

stitches of candlewick are large and the yarn bulky, it is best to work in a hoop or frame, and the extra fabric beyond the 15″ needed makes insertion into the frame possible.

Work all the stitches with two strands of the candlewick yarn, placing the stitches as suggested on the drawing. The individual French knots are drawn on the lines that they form. Try spacing them as shown. They should just touch each other, making a continuous line. If yours are too far apart or too close together, adjust the distance between them.

Fill each little circle in the border with a cluster of French knots. It should take about six to fill it neatly. Work the ribbon garland in solid **satin stitch,** then go back and place a French knot on top of the satin stitch at each small circle. A note about working the satin stitch with this coarse yarn: if it is difficult to make the two strands lie neatly beside each other without twist-

ing, try using a single strand. It is more work, but it can save time if the yarn is a particularly wiry one that has to be manipulated with every stitch.

Wash the completed embroidery to remove any traces of the transfer pencil lines. Do not wring. Roll in a heavy towel, press out excess water, and iron dry using a heavy towel under the embroidery as padding. Iron only on the wrong side of the embroidery.

Cover the cable cord with the bias strip to make a decorative cording for use in the seams, and construct a box pillow using the already cut muslin pieces (see **Pillow Construction**).

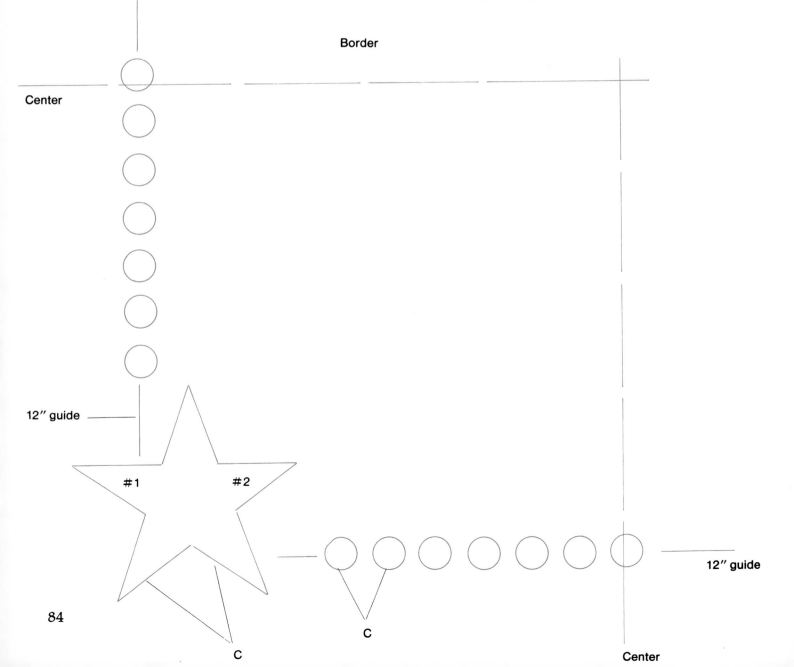

CANDLEWICK FANTASY PILLOW

When colonial women found the loom too cumbersome and limited for the creation of candlewick, they experimented with embroidery on homespun linen with a heavy cotton yarn. The French knot—and sometimes another similar knotted stitch—looked most like the raised embellishment of the woven candlewick, so it was used extensively. For special effects other stitches were added, but most of the oldest and best pieces were made with only three or four types of stitches.

Today we still like the heavy cotton yarn and use muslin to substitute for the homespun fabric. A limited number of stitches is most effective, and the French knot still predominates.

This traditional design is a good illustration of the old combination. Only four stitches are used, and the involved symmetrical design is enhanced by the extensive use of the French knot.

Size: 14″ x 14″ excluding lace

MATERIALS

muslin, 45″ wide—½ yard
cotton lace, 3″ wide, off-white—3
   yards
candlewick yarn—100 yards
chenille needle—#20
fiberfill
tracing paper
transfer pencil
embroidery hoop

INSTRUCTIONS

The drawing shows one quarter of the embroidery design, plus a small amount of design which extends across the center lines. The individual stitches are drawn, but do not bother copying them. The short lines between the French knots are there to create a line to be traced.

To make a complete drawing of the design, draw a 14″ square on tracing paper. Fold it into quarters. Open the paper flat and place it over the drawing, matching the fold lines to the slashed center lines on the drawing. Trace the quarter shown. Then fold the paper again and trace the remaining three quarters through the paper, refolding as necessary.

Cut one 18″ square and one 15″ square out of the muslin. Use the larger for the embroidery; the extra fabric will allow comfortable placement in the embroidery hoop.

Go over the drawing with a transfer pencil. Using a hot iron, transfer the design to the muslin, centering it carefully. Place the fabric in a hoop, and following the drawing for stitch placement, complete the embroidery. Use two strands of the candlewick yarn for all stitches.

The placement of **French knots** as shown on the drawing should make them close enough to be just touching each other, forming a continuous line. Adjust this placement if necessary. Fill the small heart-shaped flowers solidly with French knots. Use two rows of French knots to make the scalloped border.

Wash the completed embroidery to remove any traces of the transfer pencil. Do not wring, but roll in a heavy towel and press to remove water. Place a thick towel on the ironing board and iron dry on the wrong side; the padding will accentuate the French knots.

Trim the embroidered piece to 15″ x 15″. Gather the lace to fit around the pillow top. Pin and baste it to the top, raw edges together. Join the top and the 15″ square muslin backing in a ½″ seam, leaving part of the bottom open for turning. Trim the corners and turn right side out. Stuff with fiberfill. Close the opening.

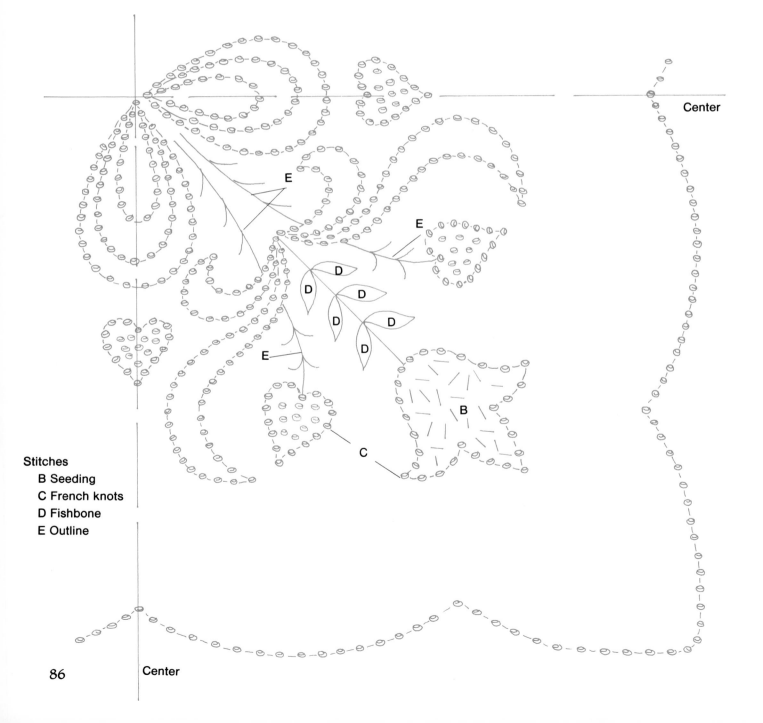

Center

Stitches
  B Seeding
  C French knots
  D Fishbone
  E Outline

Center

PRIMITIVE SWAN HOOKED RUG

It is very hard to define that elusive quality in folk art that reaches out to us and makes us lifelong collectors. Most lovers of this primitive art readily admit that they never made a conscious decision to become collectors. Suddenly one piece attracted them and that was it. They were adopted. They were inveterate collectors.

This swan weathervane was my piece. The designer may have been unschooled, but he had a wonderful understanding of line and design. Something in it "hooked" me. The rug using the swan motif is my favorite article in this book. Its simple design evokes all kinds of memories of old Pennsylvania houses filled with treasures much like it. The colors are dusty country colors that might have begun life as bright shades but have mellowed over the years to these soft tones.

Size: 23½″ x 39″

MATERIALS

#10 mono canvas—45″ x 30″
cotton fabric, 45″ wide
   colonial blue—2¾ yards
   black—1 yard
   dark green—1 yard
   medium green—1 yard
   pale green—⅓ yard
   gold—½ yard
   dark rose—½ yard
   medium rose—½ yard
   light rose—½ yard
   lavender—¾ yard
   tan—¾ yard
   navy—¾ yard
   unbleached muslin—1⅛ yards
tracing paper
fabric marking pen
rug hook
frame for rug
skid-proof backing (see page 129)

INSTRUCTIONS

Read the **Rug Hooking** chapter before

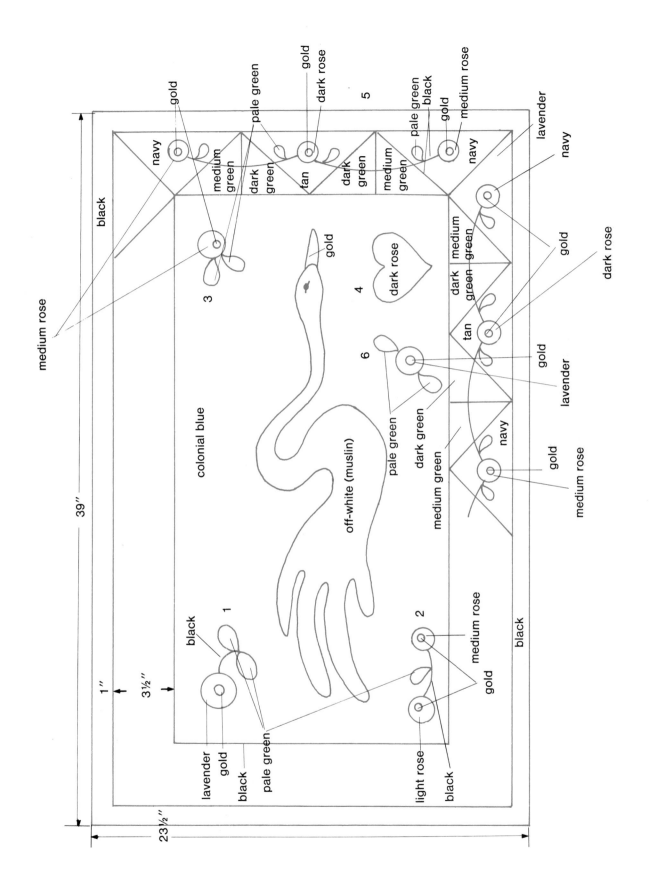

starting to work. There you will find complete instructions for washing and cutting the fabric, putting the design on canvas, and the actual hooking process.

The design elements for the rug are illustrated here full size, to be assembled on the canvas as shown in the layout. Each small motif is numbered on the drawing and on the layout to aid in matching. Use motif #3, repositioning the leaves, to create flower #6.

Make a full-size drawing of the rug. Use a large sheet of paper, piecing it if necessary. The dimensions of each portion of the rug are given on the small drawing. Draw the outline of the center field first, then build outward with the borders. Draw the triangles in the border as in the layout.

Make a separate tracing of the swan, matching the slashed vertical lines. The short horizontal lines should all line up also. Then trace the swan onto the rug pattern, centering it in the inner field. Place the center motifs (#1, #2, #3, #4) in the positions shown on the layout. The border motif (#5) is measured to fit the ends of the rug. To lengthen it for the longer sides, simply repeat one flower and two vine triangles.

Trace the completed pattern onto the rug canvas.

Hook the rug, following the layout for color placement. Note that the

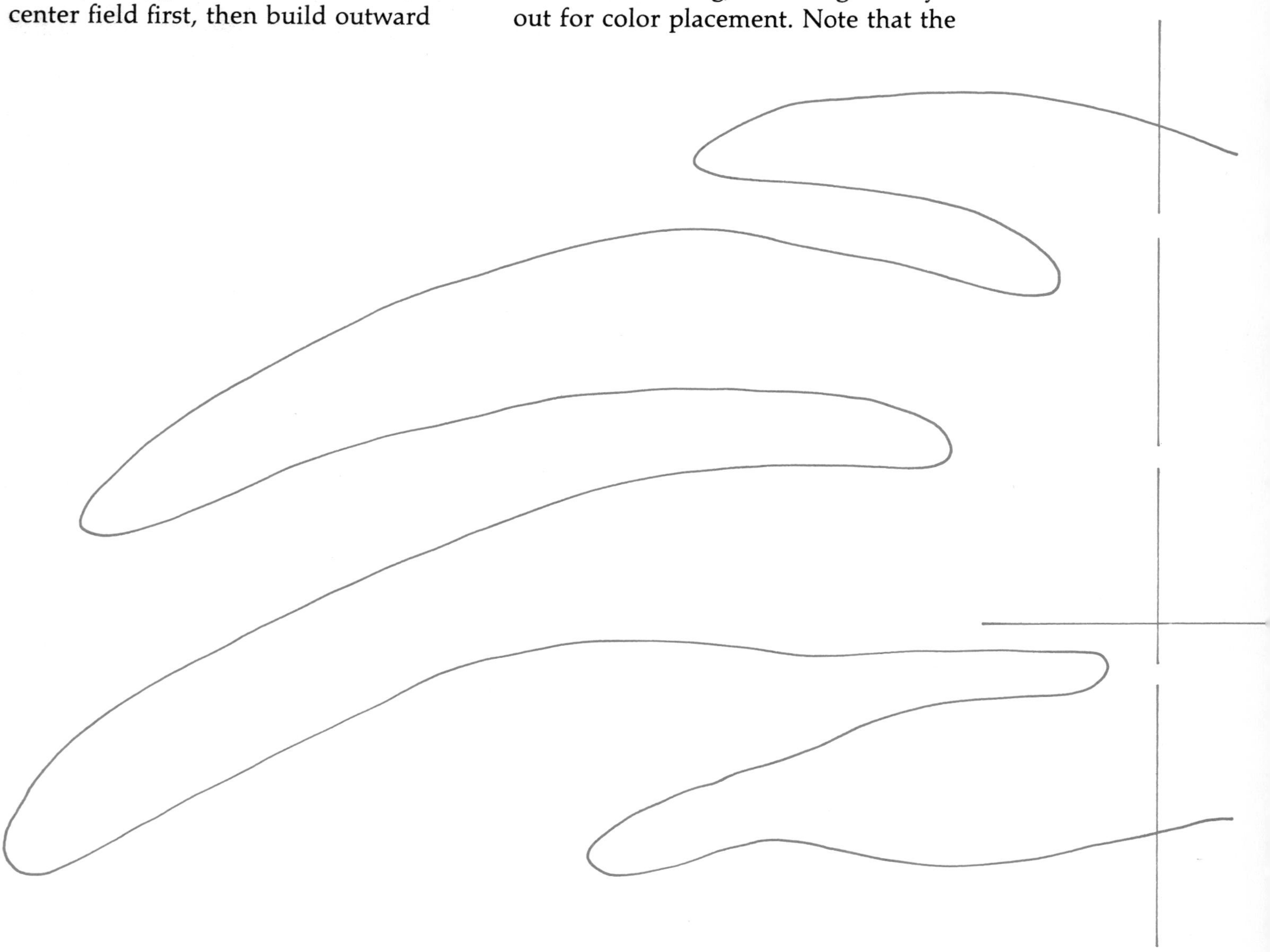

90

center field and all the triangles in the border are to be outlined with a single row of black. All the vines and stems are black, and the leaves in the border have a thin outline of black.

Follow the instructions in **Rug Hooking** for finishing and backing the rug.

This project is fun. Enjoy it! You'll soon be as attached to my swan as I am!

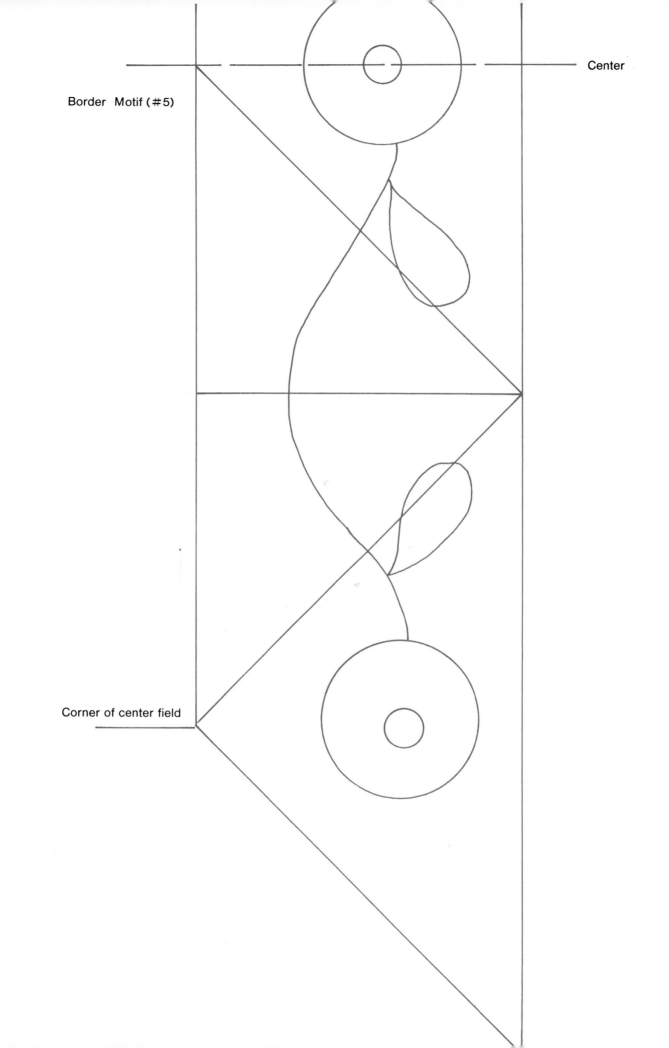

Center

Border Motif (#5)

Corner of center field

92

#1

#2

#3 #4

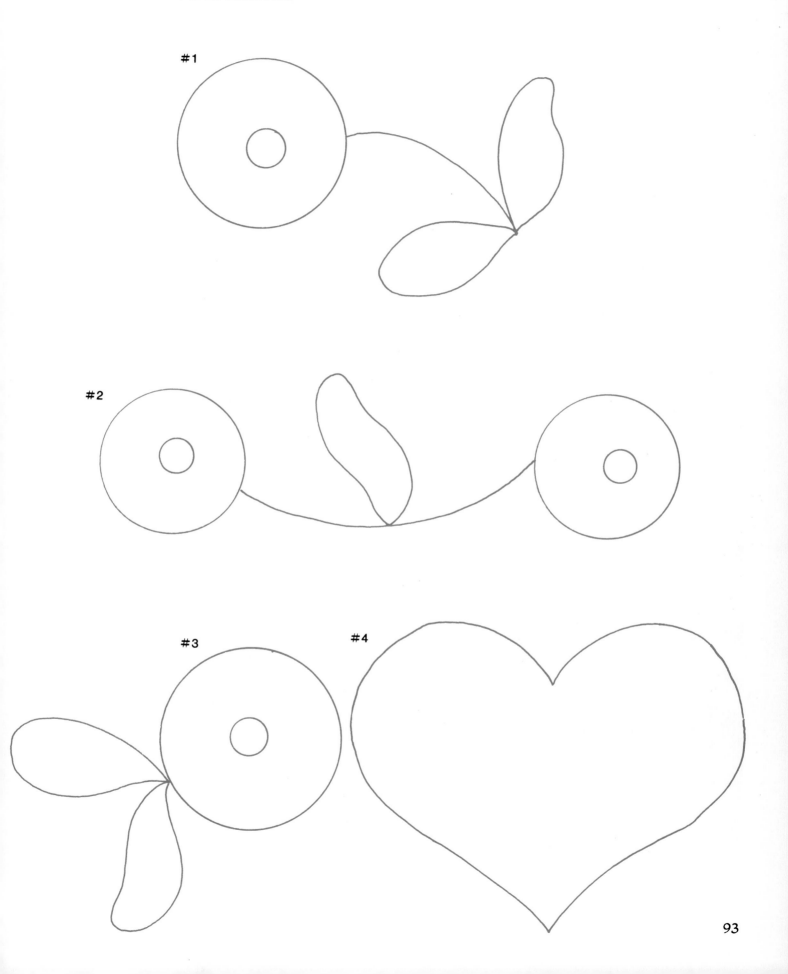

WINGED GABRIEL HOOKED RUG AND STENCILED FLOORCLOTH

Many sophisticated collectors of folk art have narrowed their acquisitions to very specific categories—one may want anything that is decorated with a heart, another goes even further and collects only iron tools that have a heart incorporated into the design. The heart must be by far the most collected of all motifs, but eagles, swans, angels, flags, and all manner of animals have found their way into folk art and are eagerly sought.

Carrying this theme through to new craft projects with a folk art flavor, we are using the graceful form of the Angel Gabriel for a cross stitch picture, a quilted pillow, a hooked rug, and a stenciled floorcloth. The drawings can be used for other projects as well to enlarge a collection.

HOOKED RUG
Size: 23" x 36"

MATERIALS

#10 mono canvas—29" x 42"
cotton fabric, 45" wide
   muslin—2¼ yards
   deep rose—1 yard
   dark green—2¼ yards
   brown—⅓ yard
   medium gold—½ yard
   bright gold—⅓ yard
   tan—1½ yards
   blue—⅓ yard
   fleshtone—⅓ yard
graph paper
tracing paper
fabric marking pen

INSTRUCTIONS

For either the hooked rug or the stenciled floorcloth a full-size drawing is needed. Note that the sizes of the two pieces are slightly different. The floorcloth is a little bit wider because the canvas cut to best advantage to that width and it seemed a shame to cut it away just to make the two exactly the same size (true folk art tradition surfacing).

Graph paper is very useful for making these drawings since it eliminates so much measuring. Large transparent sheets (24" x 36") can be purchased singly at a blueprint supply store. The cost is minor, but the convenience is great.

Following the dimensions on the layout, draw the rug borders. Trace the full-size drawing of the angel, matching the slashed lines of the components. The short horizontal lines also should all line up. Use the large piece of graph paper for the complete rug

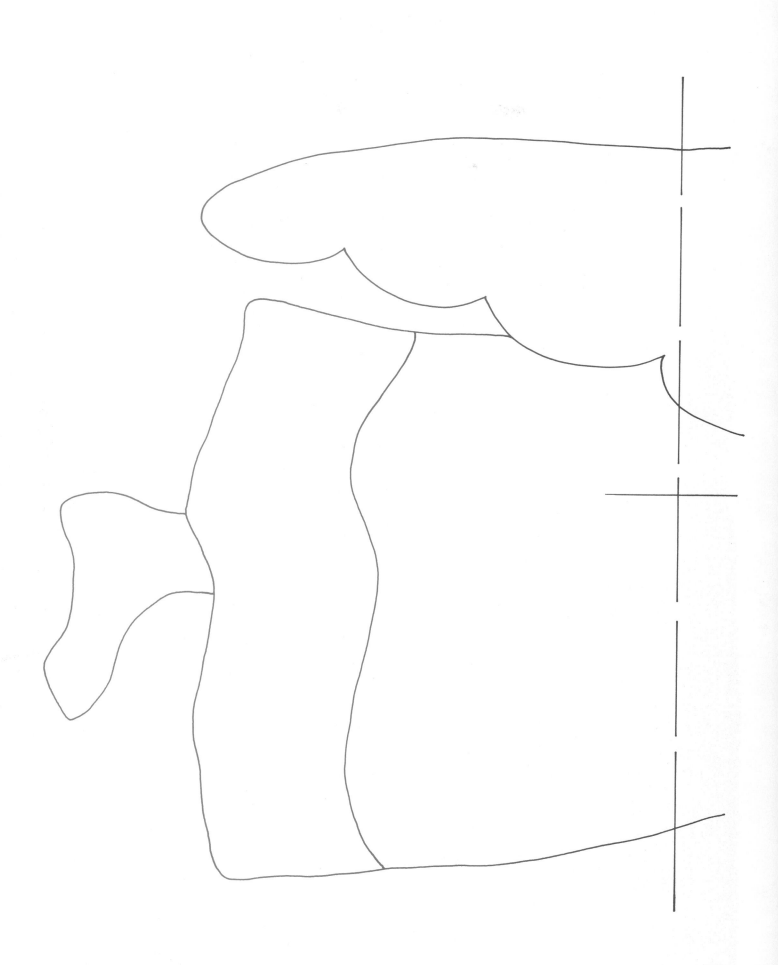

pattern. Trace the individual motifs on other paper, arrange them as shown on the small sketch, finally taping them in place or tracing them.

Center the angel on the field of the drawing. Trace the stars and date. Place these as shown on the layout. Trace the heart and make a template to repeat it on the border as shown. Make all outlines dark and heavy enough to be seen through the rug canvas.

Place the canvas over the drawing, centering it so all hems are equal, and trace the design on the canvas.

Before beginning to hook, read the chapter on **Rug Hooking** for complete instructions. Follow the color suggestions on the sketch for placement in the finished rug.

STENCILED FLOORCLOTH
Size: 26″ x 36″

MATERIALS
heavy cotton canvas, preferably presized—28″ x 38″

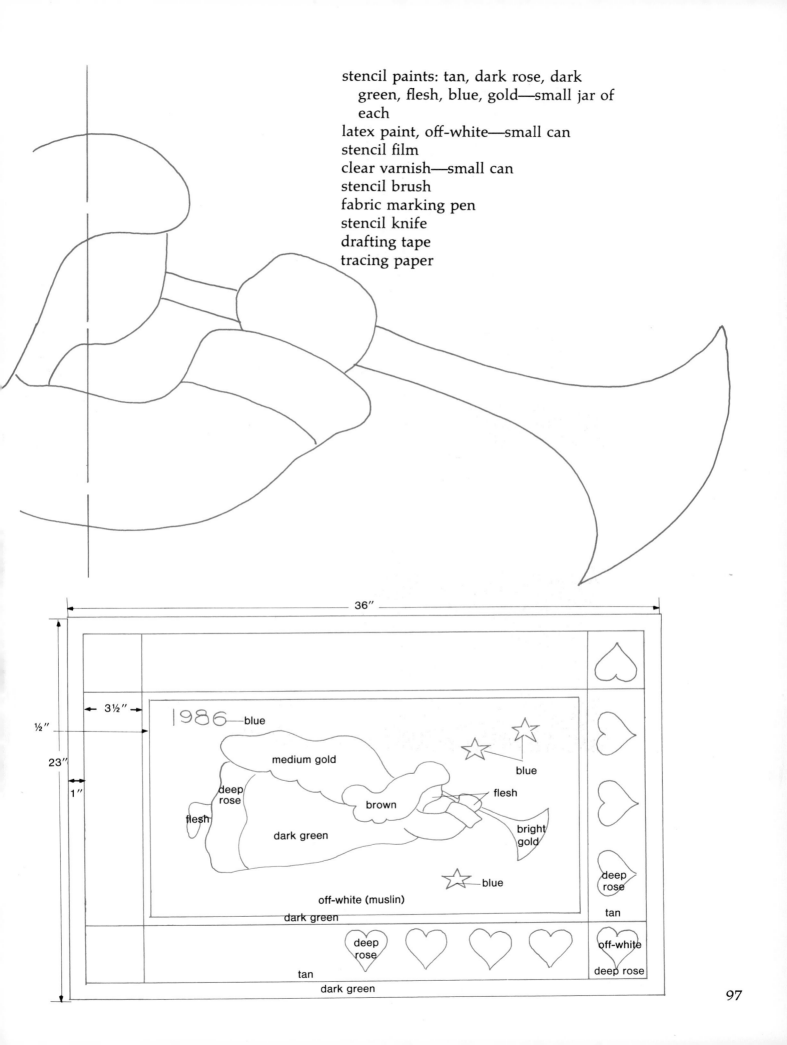

stencil paints: tan, dark rose, dark
  green, flesh, blue, gold—small jar of
  each
latex paint, off-white—small can
stencil film
clear varnish—small can
stencil brush
fabric marking pen
stencil knife
drafting tape
tracing paper

36″

3½″

½″

23″

1″

1986 —blue

medium gold

deep
rose

flesh

brown

flesh

blue

dark green

bright
gold

deep
rose

blue

off-white (muslin)

dark green

tan

deep
rose

tan

dark green

off-white

deep rose

97

INSTRUCTIONS

Cut and prepare the canvas as directed in the **Stenciling** chapter. Leaving the 1″ hem allowances unpainted, put a coat of off-white on the canvas for background color (borders will be painted over the base coat).

Use the directions for the hooked-rug version to make a full-size drawing of the floorcloth, noting that there is a 3″ difference in the widths of the two. Use either dimension, choosing the one that allows best use of the canvas. The only change that comes about as a result of the extra width is that there are four hearts on the side borders of the stenciled rug, three in the hooked one. There is also a small amount more background behind the angel in the stenciled version.

With very light pencil lines mark the borders on the canvas according to the dimensions on the layout drawing.

Then trace the design onto the stencil film. If you have a sheet of film large enough to do it, cut it the size of the center field. This makes placement easy, but if you must use smaller pieces of film, try to arrange it so that one edge touches one of the sides to help with centering. The first stencil should be the master stencil. From it cut the robe (minus hem and sleeve borders), horn, and stars. From a second piece of film cut the face, hand, foot, and wing. From a third stencil cut the angel's hair, the date, and sleeve and robe borders. Cut a border piece for the hearts.

Using tape to mask the edges, paint the borders. Stencil the hearts on the wide border, placing them as shown in the sketch. Beginning with the master stencil, paint the angel, stars, and date.

Finish the floorcloth, following the instructions on pages 141–142.

BRIDAL WREATH STENCILED FLOORCLOTH OR HOOKED RUG

Appliqué quilt patterns are a fertile source of design for both stenciled floorcloths and hooked rugs. This adaptation is suitable for either. In fact it was designed to be a hooked rug, but because of time and a manuscript deadline I decided to do the stenciled version instead.

It's nice to make a rug or floorcloth to match other accessories in a room, but either one alone is a cheerful accent and is sometimes all that is needed.

Use the stencils from the Bridal Wreath Quilted Pillow for the rug. If you have not made the pillow, check the directions on page 50 for tips on laying out the stencil. Read the **Stenciling** chapter for basic instructions as well as floorcloth specifics.
Size: 26″ x 36″

MATERIALS

heavy cotton canvas, preferably pre-sized—28″ x 38″
stencil paints: rose, green, gold—small jar of each
latex paint, off-white—small can
stencil film
clear varnish—small can
stencil knife
stencil brush
drafting tape

INSTRUCTIONS

Cut and prepare the canvas as directed in the **Stenciling** chapter.

Leaving the 1″ hem allowances unpainted, put a coat of off-white paint on the canvas for background color. The layout indicates the placement of the floral design and gives all measurements needed. With very light pencil lines, mark the borders according to the layout. (Check to make sure that any marks put on the painted background can be cleaned off. Usually lines made with soft lead pencil can be removed with a damp cloth. Check in an inconspicuous place.)

Outline both sides of the narrow inner and outer borders with drafting tape and paint these green.

Draw a horizontal and a vertical line through the rug to divide it into quarters. These will be used as guides when placing the stencils. When the line is on an area that will be stenciled, remove that part of the line before applying the color.

Working in the center of the rug, place the master stencil in position on the left portion of the field as shown in the layout. The top and bottom edges of the stencil should touch the inner border line, and the flower center at the right side of the stencil should be

centered over the point at which the lines cross. Stencil these green and gold areas. Move the stencil to the right, keeping the top and bottom edges even with the borders and placing the opening for the flower center at the left over the already stenciled flower center at the middle of the field. Stencil these gold and green areas. Note that where the two stencils overlap at the middle there is not room for one of the leaves. In true folk art tradition, simply leave it out.

Stencil the flowers.

To establish the border pattern, stencil the flowers first, then the vines, placing them as shown in the layout. Use the small leaf and vine design provided here to cut a stencil to be used between the flowers on the end borders.

Finish the floorcloth as directed on page 141–142.

To use this pattern for a hooked rug, use the same plan for laying out the design on canvas. Cut the fabric and hook as indicated in the **Rug Hooking** chapter.

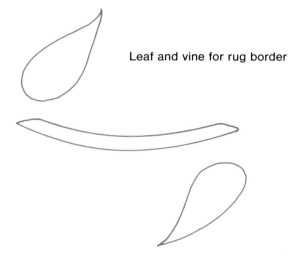

Leaf and vine for rug border

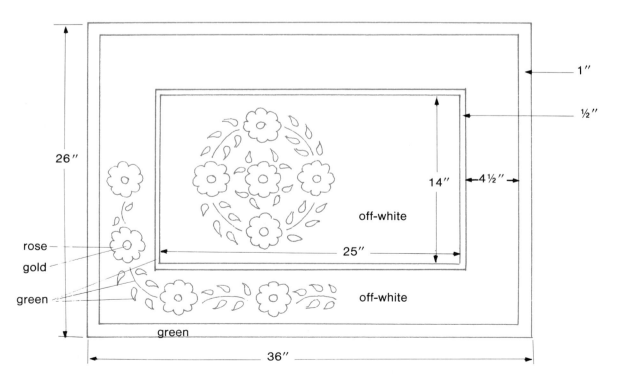

MINIATURE CROSS STITCH PICTURES

Cross stitch has won our hearts, and whimsical little pictures like the ones in this group are part of the reason. All of these are simple designs that can be framed and used together or can be used as the spark to add life to any number of other projects. Try "Love" on perforated paper or fringed linen for a bookmark for a favorite Valentine. Put the little hearts from "Home Sweet Home" on a muslin or Aida border and sew it on a towel to bring a country touch to the powder room.

The stenciled mats add another country element to the pictures and are easy to do. Drawings for the various cutouts are included so you can make your own. Pick up a color from the embroidery for a custom touch.

All four pictures were worked on an off-white linen in the floss colors noted. All were then dipped in a coffee "antiquing" solution to give them a little age. This darkened both linen and floss evenly all over. Then extra dye was painted on the still-wet fabric around the edges to darken them further.

See the chapters on **Counted Cross Stitch** and **Antiquing Fabrics** for detailed instructions.

HOME SWEET HOME

Size: 5¾″ x 8¼″ (can be matted to a standard 11″ x 14″)

MATERIALS

linen, off-white, 35 count—10″ x 13″
DMC embroidery floss, 1 skein each
   #336, dark blue
   #312, medium blue
   #676, gold
   #469, dark green
   #470, medium green
framing materials as desired

Center

Color key

336 Dark blue	
312 Medium blue	
676 Gold	
469 Dark green	
470 Medium green	

Center

Color key

⬚ (dotted)	469 Dark green
⬚ (dashed)	347 Dark red

LOVE

Size: 4¼″ x 2⅛″

MATERIALS

linen, off-white, 35 count—8″ x 6″
DMC embroidery floss, 1 skein each
    #469, dark green
    #347, dark red
framing materials as desired

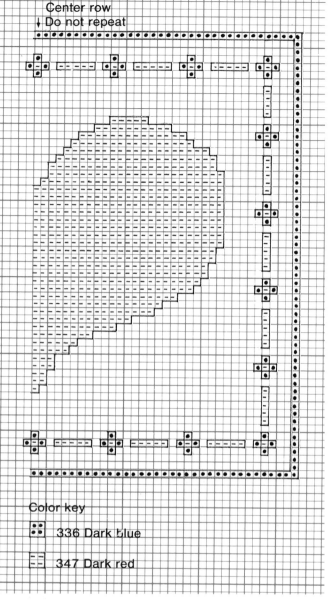

Center row
↓ Do not repeat

Color key

•• 336 Dark blue

-- 347 Dark red

MINIATURE HEART
Size: 3¼″ x 4½″

MATERIALS

linen, off-white, 35 count—6″ x 7″
DMC embroidery floss, 1 skein each
   #336, dark blue
   #347, dark red
frame and mat as shown

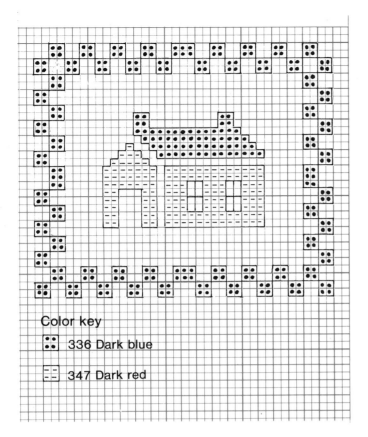

Color key

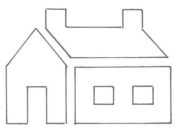

■■ 336 Dark blue

= = 347 Dark red

MINIATURE HOUSE
Size: 2¼″ x 2¾″

MATERIALS

linen, off-white, 35 count—6″ x 6″
DMC embroidery floss, 1 skein each
    #336, dark blue
    #347, dark red
framing materials as desired

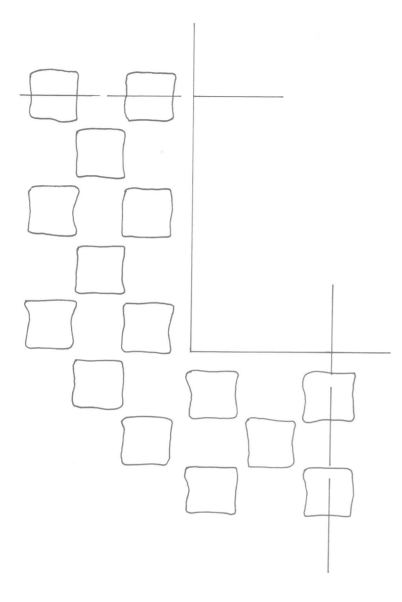

INSTRUCTIONS

Zigzag the raw edges of the linen to prevent fraying. Use two strands of embroidery floss for the **cross stitch.** The materials lists specify one skein of floss of each color for each picture since this is the smallest unit you can buy. If you decide to make all the pictures, however, one skein of each color will be sufficient for all of them.

Begin working wherever it is most convenient for you. Work each stitch over two threads horizontally and vertically. Each square on the chart represents one such stitch; remember this when counting spaces between motifs.

Work the entire design in cross stitch in the colors noted on the charts. Along the slanted rooflines of the little houses on "Home Sweet Home," work half stitches inside the lines to make the lines continuous.

Stencil patterns are included should you wish to decorate your mats like those in the photographs. This is a quick-to-do touch that really adds a country feeling.

If you wish to antique the pictures, as these were, see the directions for that process in **Antiquing Fabrics.**
Wash the completed embroidery if necessary. Rinse well in cold water to remove every trace of soap. Do not wring: roll it in a towel and squeeze out any excess water. Place a heavy towel on the ironing board and lay the piece on the towel, wrong side up. Iron dry, straightening the piece in the process. Do not apply the iron to the right side! Stretch and lace the dried piece to a firm backing. Place in a rustic frame.

WINGED GABRIEL WEATHERVANE PICTURE

The graceful form of the winged Angel Gabriel figures prominently in the list of favorite early folk art designs. Either unclothed or swathed in a flowing robe, but always with his horn, he can be found on weathervanes, inn signs, and in various other traditional forms. An early tavern sign was the inspiration for this version and the central figure of the hooked rug on page 94.

An unbleached even-weave linen makes an interesting background for this very easy cross stitch design. Each section of the angel is first outlined with outline stitch; then the interior is filled in with cross stitch. No counting!

A counted pattern like those usually found in blackwork makes a lacy, textured background for the angel while a simple checkerboard grid substitutes for a mat.

The mat may be eliminated and "Welcome" or the family name added in that space. The design can also be used for a stencil pattern to make a picture or pillow with quilted embellishment.

Size: 11″ x 13″

MATERIALS

linen, unbleached, 27 count, 18″ x 20″
DMC embroidery floss, ecru—4 skeins
DMC embroidery floss—1 skein each
   #677, light gold
   #833, medium gold
   #353, flesh
   #902, wine
   #367, grass green
   #924, blue gray
blue transfer pencil or washout pen
tracing paper
framing materials

INSTRUCTIONS

On this dark linen it is best to use either a blue transfer pencil or to trace the design onto the linen with one of the blue washout pens. To use the washout pen or pencil, first trace the oval outline and the angel with a felt-tip pen, making a heavy line. Place the drawing under the linen, taking care to center it, then trace the design onto the linen using the washout pen. If it is difficult to see through the linen even with the heavy line of the tracing, use a photographic light box or tape the paper and linen to a window and take advantage of the natural light to make the tracing.

If you prefer to use a transfer pencil, see the instructions on page 114 and the directions on the pencil package.

Zigzag around the raw edges of the linen to prevent fraying. Use three

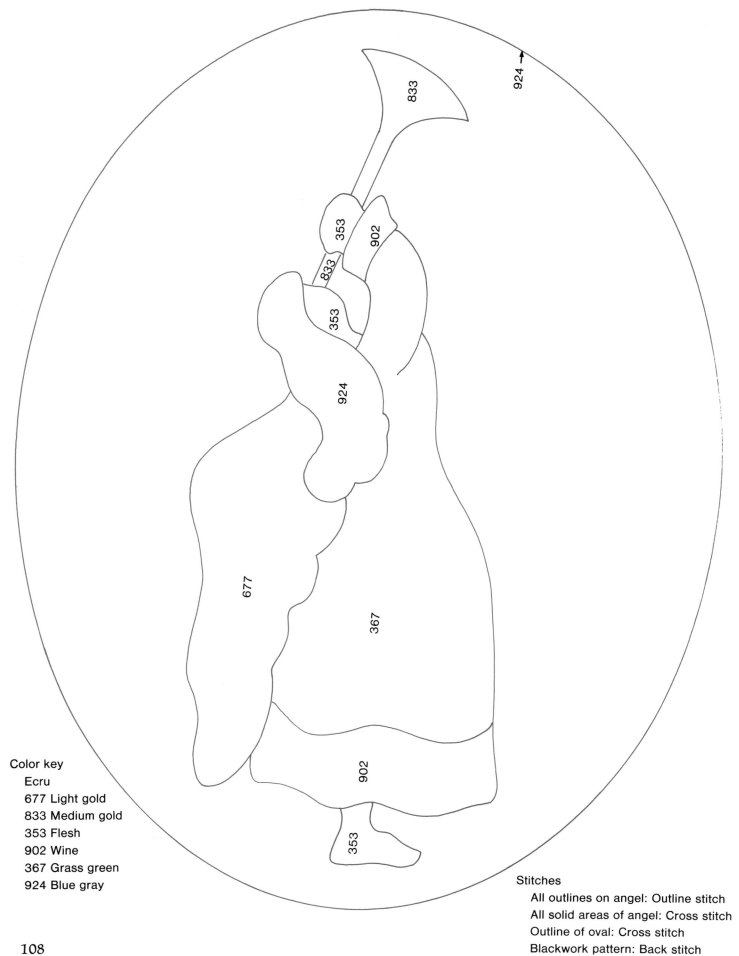

833

924

353

833

902

353

924

677

367

902

353

Color key
  Ecru
  677 Light gold
  833 Medium gold
  353 Flesh
  902 Wine
  367 Grass green
  924 Blue gray

108

Stitches
  All outlines on angel: Outline stitch
  All solid areas of angel: Cross stitch
  Outline of oval: Cross stitch
  Blackwork pattern: Back stitch
  Checked mat: Cross stitch

Work the outline of the oval in cross stitch (blue gray). The blackwork design is for the background inside the oval; work it in ecru. The checked design goes outside the oval; the pattern is worked in ecru floss. This design was also used for the stenciled and quilted pillow on page 28.

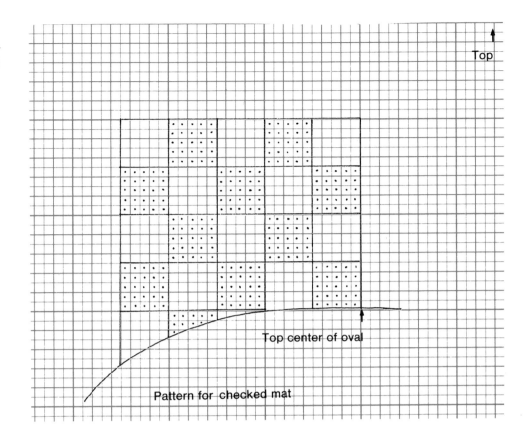

Top

Top center of oval

Pattern for checked mat

strands of floss for all outline stitch; use two strands for all cross stitch and the blackwork design.

Using **cross stitch,** work the outline of the oval with the gray floss. It really is not necessary to plot this outline on graph paper and count stitches. On linen this fine, the line will be regular enough to make a neat oval if the stitches are simply placed following the blue line as closely as possible.

Outline each section of the angel with **outline stitch** in the color indicated on the drawing, then fill in each with cross stitch in the same color. Work the cross stitches over two threads horizontally and vertically so the stitch count is approximately 13 to the inch. Fill each area as close to the outline as possible, using half stitches where necessary.

Work the blackwork design in the background of the oval with the ecru floss. Center the first row of the pattern by finding the center of the oval at the top. Mark that thread and follow it downward to where it meets the wing. Start the pattern at that point and work as many repeats as necessary to meet the gray line of the oval. Always work right to the gray cross stitches, using whatever portion of the pattern it takes at the end.

The repeats of the pattern should always align horizontally. To do this, count across twelve threads from the stitch at *1* on the chart and begin the pattern for the next row at that point with that stitch. Work as many repeats as needed to reach both the angel and the oval outline. Complete the nine rows needed to fill the top section of the oval, spacing all rows twelve threads apart. The two end rows will continue down into the lower section and establish the correct counting sequence for that portion.

The checked mat may be worked

at this point or it may be started at any time after the gray oval outline is established. Many who get bored doing large areas of regular pattern prefer to intersperse this work with time spent on the more interesting patterns. This is fine and has no effect on the completed work.

Begin working the checked mat at the top center of the oval, working four rows of squares as shown on the chart. Work in the ecru floss. Work the checked pattern to the width that will produce four squares at the top, five at the sides, and five at the bottom.

Wash the completed embroidery if necessary. Rinse well in cold water to remove every trace of soap. Do not wring: roll it in a towel and squeeze out any excess water. Place a heavy towel on the ironing board and lay the piece on the towel, wrong side up. Iron dry, straightening the piece in the process. Do not apply the iron to the right side! Stretch and lace the dried piece to a firm backing. Place in a rustic frame.

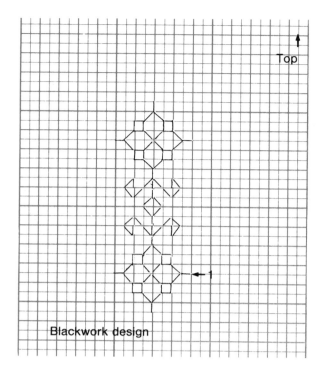

Top

Blackwork design

THE BASICS

Country needlework is easy. No involved instructions are needed to create the charming effect of old folk art pieces. The directions and information in this book are complete and allow both beginner and experienced needleworker to have some fun. Individual pieces may be reproduced exactly as described, or changes in colors, fabrics, or stitches can be made with small adjustments in the kinds and quantities of materials needed. Many suggestions for such alterations are noted within the projects themselves.

The techniques used to make these country accessories include candlewicking, counted cross stitch, Bargello, canvas embroidery (needlepoint), rug hooking, patchwork, and quilting. Stenciling and an old-fashioned method of antiquing fabrics are two additional craft ideas that help create the country look and thus find their way into the pages of this book.

The book is written much like a cookbook: after the description of each project there is a list of materials needed, a drawing or chart, and a set of detailed instructions. If the suggested "ingredients" are used and the instructions followed, the results should be a good duplication of the original item.

Read through the instructions before beginning to work. These are as detailed as each piece requires, easy to follow, and reflect my own working methods.

Good needlework and artwork depend heavily on excellence in both materials and technique. Even a beginner should not sacrifice either.

EMBROIDERY ON FABRIC

CHOOSING MATERIALS

Fabric

Each project begins with a list of the materials used for the finished model as shown. Fabric dimensions are usually noted in the exact size needed for the rather expensive linens used for cross stitch, and in approximate yards when that is appropriate for other techniques. Many shops sell even-weave linens in the small pieces suggested, saving waste and extra expense.

When yardage for a quilting or candlewicking project is specified, please note that these amounts do not include the huge overages commonly built into commercial patterns. If you know you waste material, or if you worry about shortages, you may want to buy an extra yard or so. The special fabric requirements for each category of needlework are discussed in detail under the heading for each technique.

Buy the best materials available. Good quality is one of the best investments since the work goes more smoothly and the final product is much more valuable. When the time and talent put into an embroidery project are considered, it is easy to see how unwise it is to lavish so much on unworthy materials.

Cotton Embroidery Floss

Any good reliable brand of six-strand cotton embroidery floss can be used for the cross stitch projects. Most brands are soft, easy to use, and reasonably consistent as to dye lot match (important if you run out of a color and need to buy more).

Since most of the major brands identify colors only by number, I have specified DMC brand and use their numbers in order to make exact duplication possible. Other well-known brands are equally fine; select the colors using the DMC numbers as reference on the substitution charts available in most stores.

Candlewick Yarn

This soft yarn is usually found on cards or in skeins containing convenient yardages. Since packaging varies, the total number of yards of yarn used to complete a project is given in the materials list rather than the number of skeins or cards. Divide the yardage of the package you will be using into the total to find the number of packages to buy.

These yarns are almost universally 100 percent cotton, but there is some variance in the twists: some are tight and hard, others are soft and loose. These differences do have a small effect on the embroidery, but none so serious that it requires much attention. In the project instructions it is noted that adjustment may be needed in the spacing of French knots to make a smooth line: this is caused by both the differences in the yarns and the differences in working tension.

The preferred color, and the most easily found, is the traditional off-white, but new colors have been recently introduced and do bring a new perspective to the embroidery.

Needles

Find the best-quality needles available in the type each embroidery dictates. Buy an assortment of sizes since you may prefer one different from the one specified.

Nothing is more frustrating than

having to work with the wrong needle. I have a preference for English needles, finding them usually to be of excellent quality.

Thimble
Use a thimble if you are in the habit of using one for other sewing, but do not fret if you find it more trouble than it is worth. Beautiful embroidery can be worked with or without a thimble. It is purely a matter of personal preference.

Scissors
Every sewer and embroiderer knows the importance of good scissors designed for the project at hand—and the equal importance of using those scissors only for that purpose. Find scissors with tapered points that are sharp to the very tips, and take good care of them.

Special scissors for embroidery, quilt making, and rug making are discussed in the chapters devoted to those techniques.

Transfer Pencils
These amazing new tools make it easy to apply an embroidery design to fabric. Actually what you are doing is creating your own version of the old commercial hot iron transfers. Some of these transfer pencils contain pigments that wash out easily; others must be removed with cleaning fluid. For cotton fabrics the washable kind is best. Check labels when buying and test before using. Other pencils transfer the design by mere pressure, without any heat. Most are very good, but some wear off before the embroidery is complete. Again, testing is the only way to find the product that is best for you.

Marking Pens and Pencils
There are felt-tip pens containing a blue ink which flows freely onto fabric and does not bleed: a wonderful new product. The ink disappears when

blotted with a damp cloth! Called "washout" or "disappearing-ink" pens, these have many uses.

Although I use these pens freely on many projects, I do have some reservations about them. Every mark that is put on fine fabric and embroidery must either come out or be placed where it won't be visible. The ink must not bleed into adjacent fibers or run when the piece is washed. Finally, no one knows the long-term effect of these chemicals on fabrics. The products are so new that there simply has not been enough time to see what effects, if any, are evident with age.

My solution to the dilemma is to use the pens on things I assume will have a short life and no great value. On really fine embroideries, canvas work, and heirloom sewing I avoid the pens unless I can mark in an area where I know damage won't be serious if it should occur. I find this an acceptable compromise as I really like using the pens. For most of the quick and easy instant "heirlooms" in this book I think they are fine.

Chalk or washout cloth marking pencils are also invaluable aids to needleworkers. Made in a variety of colors, they usually come in the form of thick, natural wood pencils, which can be sharpened to make as fine a line as needed and do not bleed. Lines will last until a project is completed and can be easily removed. These pencils are safe to use on most fabrics. Check labels carefully before purchasing one. There are two types which look exactly alike—one washes out, the other is permanent.

Tracing Paper
Since you will often be using your tracings of the designs for a transfer pattern as well, it is usually best to use the fairly heavy parchment or vellum

tracing paper found in pads in art supply stores. Most of these stand up to the heat of an iron and provide enough protection to prevent scorching the fabric.

TRANSFERRING DESIGNS TO FABRIC

Line drawings in the exact size of the finished embroideries are included in the instructions, so there will be no enlarging problems for those who cannot draw. Large designs have been divided into page-size sections. All these sections have slashed dividing lines, and a small portion of the adjoining design extends across the lines to facilitate joining the sections.

Some designs are divided into four quarters; others show the full center motif and one fourth of a border; still others detail portions of a large design to be joined. The instructions given for each provide you with the best method for tracing the various respective elements into a full-size working drawing.

To copy quickly and accurately a design that has been divided into four quarters and is shown on four pages, take a piece of tracing paper at least as large as the finished size of the drawing (as noted in the instructions) and fold it into quarters. Open it flat and place it over one of the sections, matching the fold lines of the paper to the slashed lines on the drawing. Lightly trace the portion of the design shown, including the parts that extend into the bordering sections. (Trace lightly so that the book is not marred by impressions left by the pencil.) Move the tracing paper to the next section, match the fold lines to the

slashed lines on the drawing, and the small overlapping portions should line up with the drawing. Trace the remainder of that section. Continue this process to complete the design.

Check the full-size tracing and make sure that lines which run from one section to the next are smooth and that the pattern is perfect. Turn the tracing over. With a sharp transfer pencil go over all the design to make a transfer pattern. (This prevents your getting a reversed image when the paper is turned over and ironed.) Work with a very sharp pencil to keep the lines fine, because they spread slightly with the heat of the iron. If you make a mistake, begin again with a clean sheet of paper since the error will transfer to the fabric and may not be in an area that will be covered with embroidery.

Make a small sample transfer and test it on a scrap of the material or a corner of the actual piece to check the iron temperature as well as the visibility of the pencil on the fabric. If fairly heavy tracing paper is used, the heat of the iron should not scorch the fabric.

Placing the transfer pencil-side down, center the pattern on the fabric, and carefully iron until the design is clear on the fabric. Move the iron carefully to avoid displacing the paper or smearing the lines.

The embroidery stitches will probably cover most of the lines, but if some traces remain after the work is completed, washing with mild soap usually removes them. Try washing the test sample. If it does not wash clean, try treating it with cleaning fluid, then washing to remove the odor.

EMBROIDERY ON CANVAS

An entire book could be written on the subject of canvas work. Indeed, I've written four or five myself and not exhausted the subject. There are only a few canvas projects in this book, and these have been worked utilizing only two basic stitches to maintain a country simplicity.

CHOOSING MATERIALS

Canvas

Several types of canvas, mesh counts, and colors have been used in the construction of the needlepoint and Bargello projects. If exact duplication of the illustrated product is desired, the canvas should meet the specifications noted in the list of materials given with the project. A change to larger or smaller mesh will alter the size of the article and will also change the yarn requirements.

Buy the best canvas available. It is easier to work and usually nets more attractive results. Look at the canvas carefully before buying. For plain needlepoint, the threads should be round and smooth. For Bargello it is best to use canvas intended especially for that work: it has a slightly rougher texture which holds the long upright threads in place. Avoid any canvas with knots in the threads, for these represent weak spots. Irregularities in the thickness of the threads affect the evenness of the stitches. An inferior canvas usually has a dull, flat appearance and an excess of sizing. Good-quality canvas will last a long time and make more valuable the many hours of work that go into a piece of needlepoint.

When planning a project allow at least a 2″ border of unworked canvas on all sides of the piece. This is not a waste of canvas; it is essential to help maintain the shape of the canvas and make blocking possible. On smaller pieces it is all right to use a smaller border if necessary, but try for 2″ if possible.

Tape the cut edges of the canvas with masking tape to prevent fraying and to keep the yarn from snagging as you work. Use only masking tape; other types work loose and sometimes leave messy sticky deposits on the canvas.

Roll the canvas to fit into your hand when you are working in the center—never crush and break the sizing deliberately so the canvas can be wadded into the hand. Puppies love to chew canvas, and all cats seem to have the idea that needlepoint projects in the making are designed just for them to sleep on. Don't tempt either by leaving your work where they can find it.

Frames

The use of a frame for needlepoint is optional. If you use one, your work is less portable and you'll have to learn to work with one hand above the frame and the other below it, but the canvas does maintain its shape and remain crisp and new. The stitches are usually very smooth and regular, but this can also be accomplished without a frame. The use of a frame is therefore purely a personal decision.

Yarns

A veritable explosion of new yarns and fibers in recent years has greatly increased the choices available to canvas workers. Most of these are best for special effects. Use the primary canvas yarn, the old standby wool needlepoint and crewel yarns, for these projects. These are usually three-ply strands that can be divided to fit a number of canvas sizes.

The yarn requirements in the instructions for each canvas project are based on Persian yarn, the familiar three-ply yarn usually used for needlepoint and crewel. The color numbers listed are for Paternayan yarn, since these yarns do not have color names. This makes substitution possible and eliminates your wondering if what I mean by "medium blue" is what you mean.

The quantities listed refer to the three-ply strand regardless of how many ply are used for the embroidery. These yardages are also exactly those used to complete the photographed project with little surplus built in. The working methods used to determine the estimates are normal ones with no special emphasis on conservation, but no material was wasted either.

Whenever possible, buy all the yarn for a project at one time. There may be a slight difference in dye lots and it can be frustrating to have to try to match new yarn to old.

Sometimes, even when the yarn is exactly that specified and the canvas meets the specifications too, some colors—dark ones especially—simply do not cover the canvas adequately. Try stitching with a looser tension. If that does not solve the problem, separate the strands of yarn to remove the twist. Put them back together and try again. If that fails, give the yarn a steam bath by placing it in a steamer over boiling water for two or three minutes.

If canvas still shows between stitches, try adding another ply—you'll need more yarn if you do this. Finally, you can remedy the situation by tinting the canvas with a *permanent* marker the same color as the yarn, but in a slightly lighter shade so you can see to work.

Other Equipment
Few embroiderers use a thimble for canvas embroidery, but it is certainly a good idea if you are more comfortable with one.

Good embroidery scissors are not a luxury. Keep a pretty little pair just for canvas work.

An assortment of sizes of tapestry needles is an essential for your workbasket. The best size to use for each piece is noted in the materials list, but individual preferences may indicate using a size larger or smaller than the one recommended.

Although there is an almost bewildering assortment of marking pens on the market, relatively few are formulated specifically for needlepoint. Choose carefully, and make sure that the ones you buy are labeled for use on canvas and fabric and that they are permanent and waterproof. It is wise to test a new marker even if it is labeled "permanent."

When drawing a design on canvas it is not necessary to make a heavy black line—in fact it is best to avoid just that, as it will show through light-colored stitches as a dirty gray shadow. Instead of black markers choose light blue, gray, pink, orange, or light green. Look for sharp points so you can draw a thin, well-defined line. The lines need be only dark enough and heavy enough to be visible.

PREPARING TO STITCH
Always cut canvas between two threads and tape the raw edges to prevent fraying.

As for the other embroideries,

full-size line drawings of the projects are included, so there will be no enlarging problems. Follow the instructions on page 114 for the fastest way to make a complete tracing of designs that have been divided onto several pages. Make a pencil tracing, then go over the tracing with a felt-tip pen to make a good dark line that can be seen through the needlepoint canvas.

Lay the completed drawing on a flat surface. Place the taped canvas over it, centering it so all margins are equal. Tape or fasten the two together so there will be no slippage, and trace the design onto the canvas with a marker.

Threading the Needle

Never wet or twist the yarn in order to thread the needle. There are three methods, one of which will work for you.

Fold Method Hold the needle between your thumb and forefinger with the eye facing you. Loop the yarn end around the needle and pull it tightly to form a fold. Holding the fold tightly, gently withdraw the needle. Still holding the fold tightly, force it through the eye of the needle.

Squeeze Method Press the end of the yarn tightly between the thumb and forefinger of one hand. With the other hand, force the eye of the needle over the tightly held yarn. With only a little practice, you will be able to fit the yarn right into the eye.

Paper Method Cut a piece of paper about 1" long and narrow enough to fit through the eye of the needle. Fold the paper in half and place the cut end of the yarn in the folded paper. Pass the folded end of the paper through the eye of the needle—the yarn will be carried through easily.

You can also buy a little wire needle threader and keep it with your work, if you prefer.

Work with comparatively short lengths of yarn to save the yarn from wearing thin. On #14 canvas a 14" to 15" strand is about right. Use shorter strands on finer-mesh canvas and a longer strand for Bargello, which "eats up" yarn fast.

If the yarn becomes twisted as you work, hold the canvas up, drop the needle, and let the yarn unwind itself. Do not continue to work with the twisted yarn; it will not cover the canvas well and the stitches will have a slightly different shape as a result of the twist.

Canvas embroidery must be worked without knots. Begin a strand of yarn by simply holding it in place on the back of the work and stitching through it until it is secured. Begin subsequent strands by pulling them through the back of the last four or five stitches worked. End a strand by pulling it through the back of four or five stitches in the row above. Never begin and end in the same group of stitches, as this pulls them too tight on the right side and causes a ridge that will not block out.

Clip all ends short to avoid tangling and to keep them from being pulled to the right side when new stitches are worked around them.

BARGELLO

Bargello is a counted canvas embroidery worked primarily in the **upright gobelin stitch,** and the basic rules for good needlepoint apply to it.

Count Bargello stitches carefully, following the chart until the pattern is established. Accuracy is essential, for very often one or just a few lines delineate a pattern and all other rows merely follow. If a mistake is made in the first row, it will carry into all subsequent rows.

Since Bargello stitches are long,

they use up yarn quickly, and so it is possible to work with a longer strand than is generally used for other needlepoint stitches. A length of 15″ to 18″ is usually comfortable. Greater lengths are hard to handle and the yarn will wear thin before it is stitched in.

Learn to work Bargello stitches with a light, even tension. The stitches lie upright on the canvas and must be loose enough to allow the yarn to "fluff" up and cover the canvas. If canvas threads are visible between stitches, either the stitches are too tight or the yarn is not bulky enough.

The stitches should lie flat on the canvas with no twisting of the yarn showing. Take time to guide the yarn into a perfect stitch every time. The smooth, even surface that results enhances the beauty of the Bargello designs.

Although rendered in black and white, the Bargello charts here look very much like the finished embroidery. Color keys indicate the colors to be used for the stitches. When a stitch crosses four lines of the background grid in the drawing, that stitch should be worked to lie over the corresponding number of canvas threads. Generally, the instructions for a particular Bargello project will point out the best place to begin stitching; notes on the charts make other helpful points.

BLOCKING CANVAS EMBROIDERY

Since most canvas work is badly out of shape when completed, wet blocking is usually the best method of straightening the work and smoothing the stitches. To wet the canvas and yarn evenly, roll the piece in a towel that has been wet in cold water and then wrung out, and let it stand overnight. The following day, remove the dampened canvas from the towel and fasten it to the blocking board, with rustproof tacks placed about 1″ apart on all four sides, pulling as necessary to straighten the sides (check with a T-square).

Leave the canvas on the board to dry thoroughly. Drying times will vary, but the piece should not be removed until it is completely dry or it will revert to its unblocked shape.

Since Bargello stitches do not pull the canvas out of shape, many completed pieces can simply be fastened to the blocking board and steamed. This is easy to do with one of the small plastic steamers made for home needleworkers. It produces enough steam to loft the wool but will not scorch or flatten the stitches. The piece dries quickly after this treatment and maintains its shape as well as a piece blocked by the wet method. (Bargello that is badly misshapen and crumpled should be blocked wet. Treat it like any other needlepoint.)

Good blocking is essential to good construction. There is no way to sew a crooked piece of needlepoint into a square pillow and no way to make a lopsided picture look right in a frame.

COUNTED CROSS STITCH

Firmly rooted in our history, counted cross stitch is beautiful and has a nostalgic appeal that makes it fit into the country decorating idiom even though it was an art practiced by most young women, not just country folk. Old samplers are lovely historical records, and since most were original designs or a collection of motifs combined in an original way by the maker, many of them have the naive appeal of folk art.

Counted cross stitch embroidery is worked on even-weave fabric. Using the threads of the fabric as a guide, the stitches are always identical in size and always in perfect alignment. It is easy. What could be simpler than making two slanted stitches that cross each other in the middle? It is classic and appealing. The recent revival of this embroidery has stimulated the needlework industry to produce once more the good linens and other fabrics that had for so long disappeared from the scene in this country.

CHOOSING MATERIALS

As in all embroideries an investment in the best of materials pays dividends, making the work easier and more pleasant. Most of the threads used are relatively inexpensive, so the total cost of a cross stitch project, even on the most expensive fabric, is really very little. Special equipment is minimal too.

Fabrics
Technically, an even-weave fabric is one in which there are the same number of warp threads and weft threads per square inch. In reality there are few fabrics in which this is absolutely true, but in most the count is so nearly equal that little difference can be detected. If the count is too much off, patterns that should work out to be square will be oblong instead.

Exciting even-weave fabrics, made of linen, cotton, polyester, wool, and blends of these fibers, are available in a rainbow of colors in addition to the classic cream, white, and unbleached favorites, and all come in the complete thread-count range. For the country look, try the linens in off-white for tea dyeing (see **Antiquing Fabrics**), as well as the dark unbleached colors. These have a wonderful homespun look that complements primitive furniture and adds an antique look to a cross stitch project.

If there is a piece of fabric on which you would like to put a cross stitch pattern but hesitate because it is an irregular weave, you can use an iron-on transfer pattern, which consists of a blank grid on which these designs may be worked. When the stitching is complete, the guide washes away. A very useful little invention.

To ensure that the finished piece is the same size as the one given in this book, buy fabric with the thread count specified in the materials list. Fewer threads per inch makes the project larger; more threads per inch reduces its size. Thread count may be denoted several ways. For example, "10 count" and "#10 linen" both mean the fabric has 10 horizontal and 10 vertical threads per square inch. To cut the fabric perfectly straight, pull a thread and cut on that line.

Threads
The most-used thread for counted cross stitch is six-strand cotton embroi-

dery floss. It is available in such a wide spectrum of colors that it seems impossible that the right shade couldn't be found with ease. Work with the number of ply indicated in the instructions.

Other threads are certainly useful for this work, including linen and silk in a variety of twists. Investigate these for special effects.

Needles

Use a small-size tapestry needle for cross stitch, one that pulls the thread through easily without making too large an opening in the fabric. On intricate designs it is sometimes helpful to have one needle for each color thread.

Scissors

Small embroidery scissors are all that is needed. You may want to keep a special pair in the box with your floss to make sure they are always handy.

COUNTING STITCHES

Counting stitches—it's not hard and it is pure magic to the beginner. The colored designs grow on the plain unmarked fabric and form a picture as you work. The embroidery is so much more beautiful than that worked on stamped crosses that you will find it impossible to accept the irregularity of the stamped work. But beware: it is addictive!

When working from the counted cross stitch charts and using even-weave fabric, note that each square on the chart represents a stitch worked over a square of two horizontal and two vertical threads. When counting the unworked spaces between motifs, be sure to allow for this.

The top stitch of every **cross stitch** must always slant in the same direction throughout an entire piece of embroidery to ensure a smooth, regular appearance. To avoid confusion about the slant of the stitches, always hold the piece in the same position. If it has selvages use them as a guide, always working on the piece with the selvages running the same way.

Two basting threads through the center of a piece—one horizontal and one vertical—are great time savers and help in the counting for placement of motifs. It is usually best to find an anchor point from which to start counting and work outward from that point. Some needleworkers prefer to begin working at the center of the piece, while others prefer to start at a top corner and proceed downward. Your method should be based on individual preference as well as on the design itself. Either method works perfectly if it is carried through to the finish.

Work complete motifs rather than trying to work across an entire row. Do not "jump" across unworked background spaces with long threads. Dark threads show through the fabric when the piece is stretched, and long threads pulled too tight may prevent the piece from being blocked flat.

Learn to work without knots. The bump caused by a knot is always apparent when a piece is stretched and framed. Begin by inserting the needle down into the fabric about 1″ from the point of the first stitch. Leave a 2″ or 3″ tail of thread on the top of the fabric. Begin stitching, holding the tail of thread for the first few stitches. Go back later, pull the tail through to the back of the work, thread it into a needle, and work it into the back of several stitches. Begin subsequent threads by running them through the back of several adjacent stitches and clipping the ends close to the fabric. End a thread also by running it through already worked stitches on the back.

Cross stitch may be worked in a hoop, but this is really not necessary and it is nice to have some kind of embroidery work that can be held and worked without a hoop. This does mean, however, that the piece will be a little rumpled when it is finished. If reasonable care is taken the embroidery piece will not be soiled, but you can wash it in mild soap to freshen it. Rinse well in cold water to remove every trace of soap. Do not wring: roll it in a towel and squeeze out any excess water. Place a heavy towel on the ironing board and lay the piece on the towel, wrong side up. Iron dry, straightening the piece in the process. Do not apply the iron to the right side!

CANDLEWICKING

Surprising as it may seem, American candlewick was originally a woven art. Rather than a craft invented by frugal pioneer women seeking to use every scrap of available fabric, it was more likely used first by wealthy plantation wives to embellish their beautifully handwoven coverlets. It is believed that most of the pieces still in existence were made by slaves in the workshops of affluent colonial landowners.

The spreads were woven of plantation-raised, -carded, and -spun linen or cotton or a blend of the two. A few looms were wide enough to allow the weaving of a spread without seams, but most were narrow, so most coverlets have one or more seams. A rare and beautiful spread on display at Gunston Hall in Virginia is 90″ wide.

The term candlewicking is probably a result of the resemblance between the softly spun roving used for the raised loops and the cotton twist used for wicks in the hand-dipped candles of the day.

To make a candlewick spread, the loom was dressed with fine cotton or linen warp thread for the basic tabby weave—the threads alternating over one, under one to create a plain fabric. At planned intervals the weaver used a long narrow reed to pick up and hold loops of the heavier roving yarn. The next tabby row held the loops securely and the reed was withdrawn to be used in the next row (or shed, as weavers call it).

The patterns thus set by the limitations of the loom were basically geometric and often adapted from patchwork. There were squares, triangles, stars, trees, baskets and, as in patchwork, an abundance of political and patriotic symbols. The colors were always those of the off-white linens and cottons in both background fabric and pattern yarn.

It didn't take long for creative needleworkers to devise a method of embroidering that would free them from the confinement of the loom and allow free-form candlewick designs. The colors remained the same, but now any kind of design could be applied to the homespun linen or cotton fabric. Embroidery thread took the place of the heavy roving, and large bulky stitches created the pattern. The French knot was the favorite since it came closest to approximating the loops of the woven pieces, but many other basic embroidery stitches were used for special effects.

A later adaptation of the candlewick process developed in the late 1920s; it was a hand-done copy of the popular machine-made chenille products of the time. In this process heavy multi-stranded yarn is basted into inexpensive cotton backing. The threads are cut into tufts, and then the piece is washed to shrink the fabric around the tufts, holding them securely. Although this process was used widely at the time, its popularity was short-lived. Pieces of this work still surface at flea markets for very reasonable prices.

Modern candlewicking closely approximates the early free embroideries of the colonial period. By far the most-used color is still the off-white of the old pieces, but variations in color have been introduced in both yarns and fabric and are very interesting. The stitches and methods are unchanged.

Because texture is so important, large bulky stitches form the backbone of candlewick, making it a very fast-moving embroidery. The materials, inexpensive cotton yarn and muslin, are easily obtainable. Candlewick is used today much the same way it was originally, primarily for home decorating projects like bedspreads, curtains, and pillows. Its revival coincides with the current appeal of the country look, making it even more interesting to the needleworker.

This is an embroidery that lends itself well to experimentation. Try adding color. Work the Colonial Eagle candlewick in the stitches suggested with the off-white yarn, but use a Williamsburg blue background instead. Stencil the President's Wreath design on muslin and outline each section of the design with French knots instead of the quilting stitch. Try shadow quilting (dark fabric cutouts under the muslin) outlined with French knots either in color or in white. There are many ways to use the candlewick to enrich your country interior.

MATERIALS

The basic materials for candlewicking are available in most fabric and craft stores.

Fabric
The traditional look for candlewick can best be duplicated with cotton muslin. If the muslin has little specks of seedpod and other dark fibers, the look is even more authentic. Although unbleached white is the most traditional, other colors may be introduced for a different effect.

Other blends of cotton and polyester can be used if they have a homespun look. Avoid blends with too high a polyester content, which tends to make the fabric too smooth and shiny.

Wash cotton fabric and dry it in a hot dryer to preshrink it before it is cut. Use a little bit of spray starch if desired when ironing it.

Yarn
Candlewick yarn is a four-ply cotton thread which is softly spun and can easily be divided to make stitches of various bulks. It is usually a lovely cream color, but recently has been introduced in many colors. These can be very interesting to use to create a look entirely different from the all-white color scheme usually associated with candlewick.

Needles
A large needle with a large eye is needed to pull the heavy thread through the fabric. The needle must make a hole large enough to accommodate the yarn and allow it to be pulled through easily. Too small a needle causes too much wear on the yarn, thinning it and producing uneven stitches. Look for large-eyed chenille or crewel needles, and get an assortment of sizes since stitches are worked with varying numbers of strands of the yarn.

Hoop
Since these stitches are so large and heavy in relation to the background fabric, it is best to work in a hoop or on an embroidery frame. Choose a large hoop so the working area is a good size and the work will not have to be moved often. Remove the hoop whenever the embroidery is put down, to prevent hoop stretch marks and to avoid mashing stitches when the hoop must be placed over finished work.

If the fabric is not cut large enough to allow for placement in a hoop, stitch fabric extensions to the sides. Cut these away when the embroidery is finished.

Scissors
A small pair of sharp embroidery scis-

sors is needed for snipping thread ends.

Transfer pencils

One of the easiest ways to place an embroidery design on fabric is with a transfer pencil. To make a hot iron transfer, simply turn over the drawing on tracing paper and go over the lines with the pencil. Note that some pencils wash out readily, whereas others need to be removed with cleaning fluid. Check the labels and test first on a scrap of the fabric, as the chemicals and dyes in the pencils react differently to different fibers. (See page 114 for more information.)

TECHNIQUE

When tracing the designs to make a full-size pattern, there is no need to draw the individual stitches. A guideline is all that is needed (the short lines between the circles representing the French knots suggest the line that is to be drawn). It is also unnecessary to copy the **trellis couching.** Either leave these open or trace just several slanted lines to establish the slant of the laid threads.

As noted above, the easiest way to put a design on fabric is to go over the drawing with a transfer pencil; following the instructions on the pencil, transfer the design to the muslin with a hot iron. Always make a slashed or dotted line outlining the outside of the design, to be used as a stitching line in construction.

Basic embroidery skills produce perfect candlewick. The stitches are probably in most embroiderers' vocabulary and the techniques needed already developed. See the diagrams in **The Stitches** to refresh your memory.

The drawings for the candlewick designs show the individual stitches to convey an idea of placement. The **French knots** are a little smaller than the actual worked stitches, but the placement is fairly accurate. Try placing them as far apart as shown on the drawings. They should just touch each other to make a continuous line. If they are too close or too far apart, adjust accordingly.

It is best to anchor the first of a line of French knots with a knot on the back (it is all right to have knots on the wrong side of candlewicking). To end the thread, take it to the wrong side of the work, make a looped knot, and work the thread back through several stitches before clipping it close to the fabric. For **satin stitch** and other solid stitches, when possible begin the thread on top with a few small stitches and cover them with the decorative stitch.

When working a line of French knots, wrap the yarn around the needle in the same direction for all knots for a smooth line. Since this twist is an automatic process, you probably already do this without thinking about it. Check yourself for a few stitches since a reverse wrap on one knot causes a bump in an otherwise neat line.

Work all stitches with a light, even tension and be careful not to pull these big stitches too tight, or the muslin will pucker.

Wash the finished embroidery to remove all traces of the transfer pencil. Rinse well but do not wring. Pick the piece up out of the water and spread it on a heavy towel. Roll it up in the towel and press out the water. Pad an ironing board with a thick towel, doubled. Lay the embroidery on the towel, wrong side up, and iron it dry. Do not touch the right side with the iron, and be careful not to scorch.

RUG HOOKING

Among the most cherished of folk art collectibles are the wonderful primitive hooked rugs made by thrifty and inventive homemakers seeking to create something of beauty while salvaging every usable scrap of fabric from worn household linens and clothing. There is a spark of creativity in each of these rugs that reaches out today, telling us volumes about the spirit of those housewife rug makers. This spark, although long ignored, has ignited new interest in these rugs on the part of leading art authorities, causing the rugs to be moved from storage rooms to museum walls, an elevation truly deserved.

Collectors use the term "hooked rug" to include several construction techniques even though some are obviously sewn and not actually hooked. Since most of the rugs were made of recycled materials, fiber content is as varied as the methods of making the rugs—some are made on burlap or canvas backing, some are wool or cotton cut into strips, others are "yarn-sewn" onto feed sacks or linen backing materials, some are clipped while others are unclipped. The variety of shapes and sizes is amazing. Most share an appealing humorous, naive artistic style. When we see one of these wonderful rugs on which the artist has drawn a cat or pig larger than the house or tree, we don't criticize the absence of perspective, but rather respond to the artist's message that the animal was of greater importance to her. So we "adopt" the frayed little rug, take it home, hang it on the wall, and think often about that special artist whose work has endured so long and continues to be cherished.

These old rugs are lovely and truly add a country ambiance wherever they are displayed, but they are scarce and unless in superb condition should no longer be used on the floor. Using the same construction methods and the same materials, it is possible to make good look-alikes that will help establish the country feeling in your home. The art of rug making is as alive today as it was in the nineteenth century, when the best rugs were made. Depending on the appearance desired, new or old fabrics can be hooked into variations or copies of old designs, antiquing added if needed, and the new rugs can begin the cycle again.

MATERIALS

Backing Fabric

The old rugs were made on a variety of different backing fabrics, depending upon what was available. Products for use today include heavy burlap, rug warp cloth, monk's cloth, and needlepoint canvas. My own favorite is an inexpensive #10 (10 threads to the inch) mono weave needlepoint canvas. After it has been washed to remove the sizing I find it the perfect backing material, pleasant to work on and long wearing. Mono canvas is a simple weave in which the threads merely cross each other without being interlocked. Don't worry about the sizing and the smoothness of weave, which are important in needlepoint. The least expensive canvas is fine.

Finish the edges of the canvas with a row of stitching to prevent fraying, then wash it by hand with soap and hot water to remove most of the sizing. Iron the canvas, and it is ready for the design.

Shown against the background of a partially hooked rug are a wood-handled hook, excellent scissors designed to clip close to the pile (the lip shields finished work), and a bunch of cotton bias strips.

Burlap is available in many grades, determined by the weight per yard. Choose a heavy firm one. Monk's cloth is more pleasant to use than burlap, but considerably more expensive. It is cotton, durable and pliable. Rug warp cloth is a heavy, stiff cotton made in several weights which make a good base for hooking.

Hooking Supplies
Since the early rugs were made largely from recycled materials, good rugs can be found in many fibers—almost any old cloth would do for a rug. Wool was preferred since cottons could often be used for patchwork, but there are some cotton rag rugs to be found. Sometimes linen is found and even silk turns up occasionally.

Therefore in the quest for authentic materials there is a great deal of latitude. Choose among those that are easy to find.

Wool Wool yarns or fabrics make lovely soft, durable rugs. If wool fabric is the choice, make sure it is tightly woven and cut it into ½″ strips on the straight grain of the material. Cutters are made especially for this task, but it is easily done with a pair of sharp scissors.

Yarn should be thick rug yarn and can be used directly from the skein. Finer yarn intended for knitting or crochet is usually too soft and tends to mat easily. Finer yarns can however be used in small amounts, especially in areas where just a small amount of a special color is needed.

Cotton The rugs pictured in this book are hooked with ½″ strips of new cotton fabric cut on the bias. Cutting on the bias creates a soft, fuzzy-edged piece that will not fray. The colors shown are from a fabric country collection that happened to suit these projects. For an older look, tea-dye your fabrics after washing them (see **Antiquing Fabrics**). The colors will be muted but still obvious.

Cotton rug yarns as well as cotton knitting yarns are really too soft to be good hooking material.

Old Materials Working to recycle materials or to create something from "nothing" is the ultimate in hooking fun. Old materials also have the advantage of already having some age on them, so antiquing is usually not needed. The most important point to remember is that it takes many strips to hook a rug, so it may be best to use found items for design areas and new material for background or other large areas.

Use only the good strong parts of old materials. Wash the item before taking it apart. Unless it is especially valuable, don't spend much time ripping out seams—just cut them out. Press the pieces and cut into hooking strips (on the bias if cotton, on the straight grain if wool). There is an amazing amount of wear left in most old clothing and household linen if worn areas are discarded. I remember as a child helping my grandmother cut up a sofa slipcover for the background of a rug. The slipcover arms were worn thin, but that rug endured for another thirty years before being lost in a move.

Old knits work up well into hooked rugs. Nylon hose should be cut a generous ½″ wide and should be cut lengthwise rather than round and round. T-shirts, sweat shirts, underwear, old blankets, felt, sheets—literally any fabric found in the home can be used with minor adjustments. This is exactly the way the early rug makers worked, so enjoy it!

Tools
Rug Hook This is a short wood handle

with a crochet-hook-type end which is used to pull the fabric up from the back of the rug. Some have a bent shank, others a straight one like the one pictured. Either works well, though the straight one is most often used.

Frame It is essential that the backing fabric be stretched tightly on a frame. Fancy rug frames are available, but an ordinary artist's stretcher frame will do. The frame does not have to be as large as the rug; the work can be moved as often as necessary during construction.

Scissors A good sharp pair of dressmaker's shears is essential for cutting strips. During the actual hooking, bent-handle rug scissors (shown in the picture) are invaluable. The shape of the handle allows the ends of strips to be cut close to the pile so they are invisible. The shaped flange on the blade protects the finished loops.

Other Odds and Ends Thumbtacks with a long shank are good for tacking the backing to the frame. A fabric cutter is handy if you are going to make an especially large rug. Other hooking methods require other tools, but the easy method described in this book recreates the old look for country homes so well that it is not necessary to invest in other equipment.

Coating Materials The construction of a hooked rug is such that if the end of a strand of material is pulled, an area can be damaged very easily. Cats and dogs and vacuum cleaners are famous for creating this kind of ravage, but a coating applied to the wrong side of the rug will prevent it.

Liquid latex intended just for this purpose can be found in craft and hobby stores. Apply it in a thin coat with an old paintbrush, taking care not to get the back of the rug too wet. Latex is washable and affords a skid-proof backing while at the same time locking in the loops. Several other products packaged for the rug industry primarily to prevent skidding also serve to fasten in the loops. Most are sold under trade names that include the word "skid."

If nothing else is to be found, coat the back of the rug with a mixture of white household glue and water. Usually the best mixture is half glue and half water, but since the glue formulas vary so much from brand to brand, it is best to test a corner before doing a whole rug. The result should be that the loops are glued against the rug back but the backing itself is not stiff. When painting on this mixture, take care not to apply so much that it wets the loops on the right side. Although they will dry, they may remain slightly darker and they will be stiff. Two light coats are better than one heavy one. See the instructions on page 131 for finishing tips when the glue mixture is used.

HOOKING METHOD

Wash and iron all fabrics to be used, whether new or used. Dry them in a hot dryer to preshrink. Treat woolens the way the finished rug will be laundered. I usually preshrink just to tighten up the weave, but that is a judgment that has to be made for each piece of fabric. The important thing is to be consistent with everything used in a rug so it can be maintained easily.

Cut the fabrics into strips. I cut wool on the straight grain and cottons on the bias. Many wools cut into ½″ strips on the bias come apart when pulled through the backing materials. Try hooking a small area and see which cut you prefer, and see if your particular fabric will stand up to the pulling if cut on the bias. It really does not affect the appearance or the wearing qualities of the rug either way.

Cut out the backing fabric, allowing at least 2″ for unworked borders. At least 1½″ are needed for hems; the extra allows space for tacking the fabric to the frame and trimming later. If possible add about 3″, but don't try to work with less than 2″. Finish the edges with either a row of zigzag stitching or bias binding to keep them from fraying.

Make a full-size pattern on tracing paper if possible. These rug designs are not complicated and require only minimal drawing or planning skills. Using a permanent-ink pen, mark the outside edges, allowing the 1½″ minimum for a hem. Draw in the line for the border if there is one, and then lay out the rest of the design. If you are using needlepoint canvas, the individual motifs can be traced with a heavy outline, then placed under the canvas and traced directly onto it. If you are using an opaque backing fabric, the motifs can be transferred using a transfer pencil and a hot iron (see page 114) or the motifs can be cut from heavy paper and these used as a guide for drawing directly on the fabric. Don't overlook the fact that all these rug motifs can be interchanged to make other interesting combinations. Also, many of the stencil designs from the quilting and candlewick sections can be used for rugs. It would be fun to make a rug to match any of those projects.

Tack the rug backing to a frame with the right side up. The frame need not be as long, but it is good if it is at least as wide as the rug—then the fabric can be attached so that one end of the rug can be hooked before it must be moved. Take care to pull the fabric tight, but keep the grain straight. A frame that is more than 12″ to 15″ on the short side makes it difficult to get at some areas to work. For the finished rugs shown, I used a 15″ x 30″ stretcher frame and found it very convenient.

The actual hooking is a very simple technique. Hold the hook in your normal working hand, the strip of fabric in the other hand below the frame. Put the hook through the mesh of the backing and catch the strip, pulling the end through to the right side. Let the end of the strip extend up about ⅝″. Repeat the hooking process, this time pulling up a loop about ⅜″ in depth. Loops can be longer or shorter if desired, but note that the yardages given in the projects here are for this length loop and will have to be adjusted if changes are made.

Making all loops the same length, hook until the end of the strip is reached. Pull the end through to the top as you did at the beginning. Start another strip and continue working. Cut the ends of the strips off close to the pile later. This can all be done when the rug is completed, or can be done as the work progresses.

Begin working by outlining a motif or a small area of background and work inward to fill in the area. Avoid working in rows except on straight edges such as the outline of a border or the edge of the rug, as the rows will show. Place the loops close enough to completely cover the backing and to support themselves. When you get to the center of a motif and think it is well covered, poke around with the tip of the hook and make sure no unworked areas remain.

It really doesn't matter where you begin to work, except that it is best to start in one area and then work out from that rather than skipping around. Plain background tends to be boring, so it is wise to alternate between that and the pattern.

Don't try to put a loop in every

intersection of canvas or fabric. The loops push against each other and stand up straight when placed appropriately close to each other, but should not be so close that they cause the rug to buckle.

Remove the completed rug from the frame. Trim the unworked borders to 1½″ and finish the edges again to keep them from fraying.

A coating to prevent the loops of the rug from being pulled out is desirable. Several options are available and are noted on page 129 in the "Materials" section. To apply the coating, lay the rug flat, wrong side up, on a paper-covered surface and paint the liquid all the way to the edges of the hooking. Wet the backs of the loops, but take care not to apply so much liquid that it seeps through to the right side of the rug.

While the coating is still wet, turn back the hems as close as possible to the last row of hooking and press them in place against the sticky backing.

Miter the corners neatly and coat the hems with a little more liquid if necessary to make them stick.

Dry the rug thoroughly. If liquid latex or a skid-proof backing has been used, the rug is finished. The white glue, however, is a little rough and a rug finished with it needs a lining or skid-proof backing. Muslin or ticking is a good choice for this. Cut it the same size as the finished rug, allowing for a small turn-back on all four sides. Fold this turn-back over and iron it down. Take some of the rubber strips that are sold for use in the bathtub, and sew or glue them in various places on the right side of the backing where they will prevent skidding. Glue the completed piece to the wrong side of the rug, fastening it just around the perimeter.

Another easy skid-proof backing can be purchased in most floor-covering stores. This thin layer of rubber can be cut to size with household shears and glued to the back of the rug.

PATCHWORK AND QUILTING

No single piece of folk art says "country" more emphatically than a beautiful old quilt hung on a wall or draped across a chair or bed. It seems that every collector of Americana wants quilts. At last they have come into their own and are recognized as the true art form they are. The best are sought out for museum collections, but even fragments, tattered used pieces, and unfinished quilts are eagerly bought.

No country collection would be complete without quilted pieces, and they can be completed with only basic knowledge of the quilt-making process.

MATERIALS

Most of the supplies needed for patchwork and quilting are ordinary sewing notions. A serious quilter keeps them in a special place or box and uses them only for quilting.

Scissors
Three pair are desirable. One must be a superior pair of dressmaker's shears to be used only for cutting fabric. A small pair is needed for clipping threads. The third pair must be sharp enough to cut accurate templates of plastic or cardboard.

Pins
The long fine-pointed pins with round plastic heads are good. Fine points make small holes in the fabric, and thread doesn't snag on the round heads. Sometimes these are labeled "quilters' pins."

Needles
Sometimes labeled "quilting needles" or "betweens," the needles are rather short and stubby with a small eye. A package of assorted sizes allows you to decide which is most comfortable for you.

Piecing is usually done with a "sharps" in a size that works easily on the particular fabric being used. Again, an assortment is a good idea.

Thread
Quilting thread is readily available and is slightly heavier and stronger than most sewing threads. White and off-white are good colors for most projects. Colored threads are interesting, but since they accentuate the stitches, especially when dark threads are used on light fabrics and vice versa, it is inadvisable to use them unless one is able to sew very even small stitches.

Piecing can be done with ordinary sewing thread. Some experts use only white or off-white, while others match the colors of the fabric as closely as possible. This is sometimes difficult when many differently colored pieces are being joined. If the stitches are sufficiently small and the tension correct, off-white thread usually doesn't show.

Markers
An assortment of marking tools is needed since several kinds of guides must be placed on the fabrics. Check anything you plan to use for marking to determine its effect on the finished quilt. Caution in the beginning stage often saves heartbreak later.

Several new products make life easier for the quilter. One is a felt-tip pen with a blue ink which flows freely onto fabric and does not bleed. A further advantage of this pen is that the marks can be removed by blotting them with a damp cloth. Variously labeled as "washout" or "disappearing-ink" pens, these are excellent for marking quilting lines. A word of caution about another type of pen which usually has a deeper blue ink that automatically disappears in a day or so: Don't buy this one unless you are a fast worker! There is also a pencil with a washout lead that can be used for marking quilting lines. See page 113 for more information about this pencil.

A hard lead pencil with a very sharp point is usually best for making marks on the wrong side of the fabric, especially for tracing templates. Some ballpoint pens may be used, but they should be carefully checked to make sure they do not bleed through to the right side of the fabric or bleed into adjacent light colors when the quilt top is washed.

Beeswax
A little plastic container of beeswax is a good addition to any sewing kit, and for the quilter it is especially useful. Thread pulled across it tangles less, making stitching faster and smoother.

Miscellaneous
Other equipment needed in a quilter's box includes: ruler, pincushion, seam ripper, and thimble.

Fabrics
A trip to a quilting shop is a visual delight. In the past few years the vogue for polyester fabrics for sewing virtually eliminated cotton, so the recent revival of 100 percent cotton fabrics in a wonderful array of colors and prints has been greeted by quilters with great enthusiasm. Shops further entice needleworkers by carefully arranging and displaying the fabrics in color groupings that make the quilter tingle with excitement.

Many quilting shops cater to their customers' needs by cutting fabrics into neat quarter-yard pieces that measure 18″ x 22½″. These can be cut to greater advantage than a swatch 9″ wide across the 45″ width of the fabric. Given an appropriate name like "Quilter's Sample" or "Fat Quarter," these allow the buyer to collect an assortment of prints and colors without too large an investment.

As a general rule all fabrics in a project should be the same weight and have the same care requirements. I prefer to use all cotton. I like the way cotton handles, the way it looks, the way the needle glides through it, and I feel confident about its lasting qualities.

Naturally when a number of colors and prints are to be combined, as in a patchwork design, all must be colorfast. Most new fabrics are safe, but it is wise to test before beginning to work. Preshrink cotton before cutting. If a number of small remnants are to be tested, soak each 20 minutes in very hot water. Clear water indicates that the fabric is colorfast. Finally wash the fabrics in the machine with hot water, soap, and softener. Dry in the dryer to preshrink. Press, using some spray starch if desired to replace the washed-out sizing.

Quilt Fillers: Batting and Fleece
Polyester batting is the commonest filler and is very easy to use. Most is glazed, which gives it a shiny finish and helps hold the fibers in place. For the small pieces in this book the standard thickness—not the extra fluffy— is best. If very tiny stitches are your aim, look for the new very thin batting which creates the look of the old quilts with thin cotton filler that allowed small stitches.

Quilting fleece is also polyester. It is less bulky than batting but is very good for small projects like pillows. It is like a thick felt, inexpensive and very easy to quilt.

Templates

Skilled quilters use a number of different materials for templates. Depending upon the project, cardboard, plastic, sandpaper, index cards, or poster board may be used.

Plastic made expressly for templates is very good. It is transparent, allowing one to see the pattern of the fabric, yet strong and fairly easy to cut with a pair of sharp shears. The edges stay sharp, allowing one template to be used over and over again.

To make a template from plastic, place it over the drawing and with a ruler and pen trace the quilt piece onto the plastic. Make one template for each shape that is needed. Cut the templates carefully and check the accuracy by matching them to the drawing.

Quilters disagree on whether seam allowances should be included on the templates. I have shown them on some of the drawings for those who are accustomed to using them, but I feel it is much easier to sew patchwork pieces together accurately if the template is cut without the allowances. The line drawn on the fabric is then the important stitching line. If one sews on the seam lines and matches these carefully,

a slight irregularity in the cutting of the seam allowance is not a catastrophe. Therefore it is my recommendation that templates be cut without seam allowances.

To cut patchwork pieces, lay the template on the wrong side of the fabric and with a very sharp pencil draw the outline of the template. Keep the pencil upright and keep the line as close as possible to the edge of the template. Be very careful at the corners, as these are the most important points when joining the patches. Avoid a tendency to enlarge the pieces even slightly around the edges. Pieces must be exactly alike or they will not fit together neatly.

The lines drawn on the fabric are the stitching lines; seam allowances must be added. The drawing here shows the placement of the template to cut patches allowing for ¼" seam allowances and requiring a minimum amount of cutting. Place the template so there is always ½" between the outlines in each direction. Then cut the patches halfway between the lines, and automatically there will be a ¼" seam allowance.

Use the directional arrows on the template drawings as an aid in placing

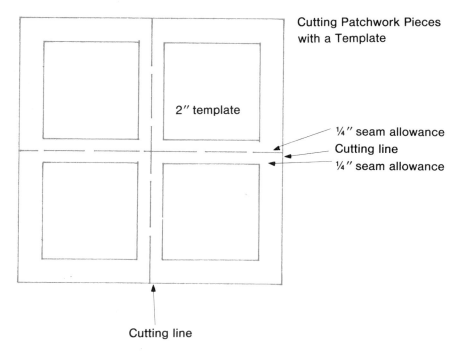

Use a template to draw stitching lines on the wrong side of the fabric, always leaving ½" between repeats. When patches are cut apart on the indicated cutting line, ¼" seam allowances are made.

Cutting Patchwork Pieces with a Template

2" template

¼" seam allowance
Cutting line
¼" seam allowance

Cutting line

straight edges on the straight grain of the fabric. Cut squares with all edges on straight grain; cut triangles as the directional arrows on the template indicate.

Cut all the necessary pieces as directed in the instructions. On a flat surface where you can leave them undisturbed until they are sewn together, lay out the patchwork pieces to form the design. Now it is possible to see how the patches fit together to form rows, which in turn fit together to make the square.

For instance, look at the diagram for the Ohio Star Quilted Pillow on page 32. Disregard the outer frame and visualize the drawing as quilt pieces laid out on a table. It is apparent that the square can be divided into three strips, either vertically or horizontally. If one chooses to work in three horizontal strips, the first step would be to join the four triangles in the top row to make the center square of that row. Next the square at either side would be sewn to the pieced square to form the row. The middle strip is constructed following this procedure, and finally the bottom strip. All should be pressed, then joined in proper sequence. Most pieced designs go together in a similar manner, whether more complicated or not.

QUILTING TECHNIQUES

Joining Pieces Together

Pieces may be sewn together by hand or by machine, but hand sewing usually results in a more perfectly joined quilt top. Use a simple **running stitch,** making six to nine stitches to the inch. Begin stitching exactly on the seam line at the corner and end exactly on the line at the other side, making the first and last stitches firm **back stitches**. Also make a back stitch each time the thread is pulled through and

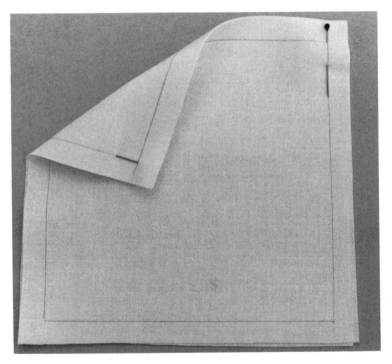

the needle inserted for the next group of stitches. This places a back stitch, which is strong, between every four to five stitches and greatly enhances the strength of the construction. This may sound like a lot of work just to stitch two little pieces of fabric together, but with practice the back stitch becomes automatic, and it is really strong. Placing the first and last stitches at the seam lines leaves all the seam allowances free.

It is not necessary to baste two patches together before sewing. Two pins hold two 2″ patches in perfect alignment, matching the seam lines and corners. Hold the two patches right sides together. Insert a pin in one of the top corners exactly at the point at which the stitching lines meet. Look at the back to make certain that the point of the pin comes through the back piece exactly at the corner. Bring the point of the pin to the top again. The pin should come out again on the stitching line (see photograph). Repeat at the other corner. After pinning several pieces you will find you can pin only the left corner and use the needle and first stitch to anchor the beginning stitch on the right corner.

Join the row of squares in the same manner, pinning each corner to match it perfectly to the row above and using the combination of running and back stitch. Strengthen the corners of the patches by reinforcing them with a back stitch as before, and instead of stitching the seam allowances flat, pass the needle through them so they stand free. This allows you to press them in any direction.

Generally it is best to press the seams toward the darker areas. Press well on the wrong side and lightly on the right side.

Adding Quilting Lines

If the project is one composed of small squares and triangles like the Patchwork Cat, it is not necessary to mark quilting lines since the quilting should be simply a line of stitches placed ¼″ inside the seam lines and following the shapes of the patches. It takes only a few minutes to get the feel of where to put these stitches, and the seam line acts as a guide to placing the straight lines.

Other quilting lines may be added with a washout pen or pencil. Sometimes it is easiest to cut a template and trace around it; other times, it may be best to use a ruler and lay out the lines according to a pattern suggested by the drawing. When quilting on the seam, use it as a guide for stitch placement. Make any marks for quilting before the finished top is layered with the backing and batting.

When instructed to quilt around motifs as in a stenciled design, simply place a row of stitches around the colored areas, following the outline closely and placing the stitches on the muslin rather than on the painted part. This row of stitches puffs up the design and really gives it life.

Assembling the Quilt

Make a sandwich of the completed top, batting, and backing. Always cut the batting and backing several inches larger than the top. Quilting changes the tension slightly in the layers and sometimes results in one being "taken up" more than the others. It's best to play it safe and trim away the excess later.

The most commonly used method of combining the top, backing, and filler is to place the three layers on a flat surface with the backing on the bottom, wrong side up. The next layer is the batting, followed by the top, right side up. Smooth out any wrinkles or bulges and pin the layers together. Baste them with long stitches working back and forth in rows about 2" apart. Leave the uneven edges.

When a special project requires a method of constructing the sandwich different from that given here, it is explained in the instructions. Although the methods are not really different (all entail layering top, batting, and backing), these slight alterations will make finishing that project easier.

Quilting

Large pieces and really fine examples should ideally be placed in a frame and quilted. Smaller pieces like pillow tops may be quilted in a hoop or in the hand so long as the basting is secure. This makes the quilting a pleasant little task that can be carried about and finished at odd moments. Baste well and enjoy quilting these little projects.

The crib quilt is the largest project that can be attempted without a frame or hoop. Be very careful not to allow the backing to pull or shift. Again, if you baste carefully, you will enjoy quilting this way.

The quilting stitch is the running stitch, simplest of all stitches. Try to make about six stitches to the inch. With more skill and a thin batting material, nine or ten to the inch are possible but not really essential on these small decorative accents. Even stitches and even tension are the goal. Stitch through all three layers, trying to make the stitches as even on the back as on the front. Whenever possible begin quilting in the center of a project and work out toward the edges.

Knots should never show on either the right or the wrong side of the work. A technique known as "burying the knot" takes care of the ends both beginning and ending.

When you begin stitching, thread the needle with an 18" to 20" length of thread and run it across the beeswax. Make a knot in one end of the thread. Insert the needle into the quilt top about an inch from where the first stitch is going to be. Go just under the quilt top, not down into the batting, and bring the needle to the surface at the point where the first stitch is to be. Pull the thread through until the knot is taut against the quilt top. Gently pull on the thread while working against the knot with your other thumb until the knot slips through the fabric. Give the thread another pull and the knot will move into position under the point at which the thread leaves the fabric on the quilting line. Begin stitching. Gather three or four stitches, through all the layers, on the needle before pulling the thread through. Pull the thread enough to compress the three layers slightly, forming a little depression along the stitching line, but not so tightly that the piece is puckered along the line. Practice establishes a stitching rhythm and tension becomes automatic.

Secure the knot at the end of a thread the way you did at the beginning, just reversed. Stitch until there are 3" to 4" of thread left. Make a simple overhand knot in the thread. Don't tighten the knot. Work it down to a point on the thread which is about one stitch length from the point at which the thread comes out of the fabric. Tighten the knot. Insert the needle where it would enter for the next stitch but do not go down through the batting. Keep the needle just under the quilt top and bring it up about an inch away, pulling the knot to the inside. Cut the thread off level with the fabric. The end falls back inside.

Trim away the excess batting and backing when all the quilting is complete.

STENCILING

Moses Eaton, the nineteenth-century itinerant stenciler who left a legacy of his work on the walls of Northeastern homes, would not be surprised by the fervor of the stencil revival today, for it is just as lovely and practical a decoration as it was in his day when he and his father, Moses, Sr., traveled from town to town carrying tool kits, pigments, and a roll of designs. For room and board, or perhaps payment in the form of farm crops, he would contract to decorate home or tavern in his own exuberant manner, transforming dull whitewashed walls with a wash of gray, raspberry, or ochre and trimming them with stencils in a combination of his favorite colors.

Having no formal art training—he learned his craft from his father—Eaton was not restrained by the rules that dictate accurate measuring, spacing, and planning, so when he reached a corner and found that his pattern did not fit, he simply used another that did or repeated a portion of pattern out of sequence. The results were charming and so distinctively his own that when one walks into one of those rooms one knows instinctively that Eaton stenciled it.

Although beautiful imported wallpaper was available at the time Eaton was working, it was comparatively rare and very expensive. Stenciled walls allowed less affluent country people to have similarly bright, attractive walls as well as decorated furniture, curtains, and bed linens. Today, as in the past, we use stencils on literally anything that will take paint. One can trim a wall using a perfect copy of Eaton's patterns and his flat opaque painting style and adding some antiquing to create an authentic background for country antiques, or one can quickly and easily add a simple border worked in today's shaded method.

Eaton's stencil box containing his brushes and his collection of stencils has survived as a result of his family's New England farsightedness. His brushes bear a striking resemblance to the ones we use today, and his stencils, cut from heavy paper or metal, though cumbersome and crude are really not that much different from ours. His paints, however, made as they were from a mixture of skimmed milk, dried pigments, oils, and chalk or lime, were much more difficult to use than the wonderful array from which we can choose. Plastic stencil sheets, good brushes, and these excellent paints make stenciling a craft anyone can enjoy today.

MATERIALS

Paint

Buy quick-drying stencil paint. Available in either acrylic or japan formulas, these are packaged in small quantities in a wide range of colors which can be used directly from the jar or can be mixed for special effects. Acrylic has the advantage that it can be cleaned up with warm water and soap and needs no special thinners. Both types dry quickly and are formulated to be the right consistency for stenciling, so if instructions are followed, there will be a minimum of problems.

It is possible to use latex wall paints for stenciling, but usually these are too thin and leak under the stencil. Some stencilers like to use tubes of artists' acrylic paints and these do perform well, drying quickly and blending easily. Experiment with thinning to get just the right consistency—too much thinner and the paint will run under the stencil, too little and it will be hard to apply the paint.

For stenciling on fabric there are specially formulated paints or dyes. If you are working only on fabric, it is best to use one of these, but if the project involves using the same design and color on both fabric and hard surface, the paint intended for the walls can be successfully used on both. Check the paint label for instructions on setting the design after painting is complete.

Stencils

The best stencils are cut from Mylar or acetate film. Easy to cut and transparent, they are durable enough to last through many usings. There is also an interesting material called "frisket," which commercial artists use frequently. This clear plastic has a tacky back that adheres to the surface being painted and thus eliminates taping on small projects.

Cutting Tools

For the average crafter a small hobby knife with a sharp blade is probably the only cutting tool needed. Buy several differently shaped blades and see which is best for you. Remember to change the blade often.

A new electric stencil cutter makes the work very easy and cuts small openings nicely, but its use takes a good deal of practice and the cost is probably more than most would want to invest.

Fine sandpaper or an emery board is handy for smoothing any rough edges on the cut stencil. A paper punch cuts tiny round circles with dispatch.

Brushes

The stencil brush has a distinct blunt shape, and natural bristles perform best, holding the paint well and wearing longer. Many sizes are available and it is best to have a brush for each color being used.

General Supplies

Tape measure, yardstick, plumb line, newsprint, scissors, tracing paper, hobby knife, drafting tape, paper plates or other disposable palettes, glass or plastic cutting mat, pencil, permanent-ink pen, turpentine or mineral spirits for cleanup of oil-base paints, "T" pins or thumbtacks to hold fabric in place.

CUTTING A STENCIL

Make a complete drawing of the design on tracing paper. If one quarter of the design is shown, fold the paper into quarters, then open it flat and lay it over the page, matching the fold lines to the slashed lines on the drawing. Trace the portion of pattern in one section of the paper. Refold the paper and trace the other three parts of the design from the copied one. Open the paper to see the complete design. If half of a design is shown, fold the paper in half and proceed in a similar manner.

Using a pen with permanent ink, trace the design onto a sheet of stencil film. Place the design on the film in a manner that will make the film itself useful in placing the designs. When possible, center the design both vertically and horizontally. Two lines dividing the sheet into quarters are helpful in this. I also cut notches in the edge of the film marking those lines, just in case the lines eventually wash away. Always leave at least 1" of film beyond the design to keep paint from smearing onto the background.

When placing a design for stenciling a border, plan to use the edge of the film as a straightedge while painting. If the border is to be 1″ below the ceiling or molding, for example, place the design 1″ from the edge of the film.

A separate stencil is needed for each color to be used. Always draw part of the motif for the other color so that the new color will be placed properly.

Practice cutting a sample stencil. Place the film on a glass or plastic cutting surface. Holding the hobby knife as a pencil is held, and always working toward yourself, begin to cut. Do not lift the knife until an entire motif is cut. Use your free hand to slowly turn the film rather than moving the knife. Hold the knife as steady as possible and cut exactly on the inked lines. Don't worry about slight irregularities—they add to the country charm.

If there are small snags or rough marks on the cut edges, smooth them out with the sandpaper or emery board.

PRACTICING THE DRY BRUSH METHOD

If special paint colors are to be mixed, prepare enough at one time to finish the entire project. Divide them into small containers to make handling them easier.

Although it is tempting to plunge right in and begin painting, take time to practice several images on newsprint. This allows you to get the feel of the brush and sometimes reveals problems with color choice or with the cutting of the stencil itself.

Inexpensive, uncoated paper plates make excellent palettes. Pour a small amount of paint onto a plate. Holding the brush upright, dip just the tips of the bristles into the paint. Still holding it upright, work the brush in a circular motion on a clean spot on the plate. Rub in this manner until all the little globs of paint disappear. In

the case of a poorly done job, the problem usually is that the paint was not worked out long enough. You need an almost dry brush to get a perfect image.

Try a sample, using newsprint or other paper. Tape the stencil in place, using drafting tape rather than masking tape to hold it. This tape leaves little residue and is easy to remove and reuse. Avoid cellophane tapes and others not meant for this kind of work, for they may pick up background paint or leave a gummy mess when moved. Anchor the stencil with only a couple of pieces of tape at top and bottom.

Use the fingers of your free hand to hold the cut edges of the design against the surface so there will be no run-under and the edges will be sharp. Begin painting, working in a circular motion from the cut edges toward the center of the image. To shade, work over the edges until the color there is heavier than in the center. Of course you can have a solid (unshaded) image if that is the style you wish. Just continue working until the coat of paint is established.

After repeated use paint will build up on the edges of the stencil. Take the time to stop and clean them before the lines of the design are affected.

Usually the largest portion of the design, the one that establishes the pattern, is applied first. A fast, well-organized stenciler working on a large project usually paints all of one color first, following with the second and finishing up with the last little bits at the end. Most of us, however, can't wait to see what the final look will be and have to finish a small portion immediately. This is fine. Work any way that makes you happy. Stenciling is adaptable to our whims—which may be one reason why we love it so much.

Once you get an image on the newsprint that looks the way you envisioned it, begin your project.

STENCILING ON FABRIC

Choose a good firmly woven fabric without nap, such as muslin, and wash and preshrink it but do not starch it (see page 133). Most of us assume stenciling works best on plain weaves and light colors, but don't be afraid to try small prints, checks, and dark colors. On the prints, the pattern will show faintly through the paint, making a pleasing texture.

Both natural fibers and blends take stencil paint well. Just to be safe, check the label to make sure the paint will work on your fabric.

Use the stencil technique described on page 140. Work on an old drawing board or something similar that won't be ruined by tack marks. Place a sheet of newsprint on the board, then the fabric, right side up. Tack in place with "T" pins or thumbtacks. It is especially important to use a dry brush on fabric. Take care not to get so much paint on the fabric that it feels wet.

Allow painted fabric to dry overnight before sewing or quilting. Check the paint jar for directions on curing the stenciling so it will be washable. Some are set by ironing, some by heating in the dryer or oven.

STENCILING ON WALLS OR OTHER PAINTED SURFACES

Plan!!! Moses Eaton just started painting and worked out problems as he came to them. You won't be happy with that unless you are trying to recreate one of his rooms.

Make all guidelines on the wall (or other surfaces where you will be applying your stencil) very light so they can be removed without trace. If a guideline falls within an area to be painted, remove it before applying any paint; if you don't, it will show through the paint and then can never be removed. Keep some of your background paint handy for repairing mistakes.

After practicing on newsprint, try the first stencil in an inconspicuous area. Lift the stencil and check the image. If it is too light, replace the stencil and go over it again. Check for run-under since the wall surface is not as porous as the newsprint. If run-under is a problem, scrub more paint out of the brush onto the paper plate until you can get a perfect print.

There is a limit to the length of time one can work accurately while standing on a ladder, crawling along a baseboard, or in one of the other odd positions often necessary when stenciling a room, so don't try to finish in one session. One big advantage to using the acrylic stencil paints is that cleanup is quick and easy, making it feasible to work for short periods of time. This is meant to be fun, so relax and enjoy it rather than trying to finish in record time.

STENCILING A FLOORCLOTH

Although any good, heavy, natural cotton duck canvas is suitable for a floorcloth, I always buy one that has been presized, saving myself that step. Some are treated on one side only, and several meant expressly for this purpose are now coated on both sides, making an excellent foundation for these decorative floor coverings.

Be certain there are no creases in the canvas, and don't let the store clerk fold it. Those creases are sometimes impossible to get out, although small ripples can be ironed out. When measuring, allow a minimum of 1″ on all sides for a hem.

Make a full-size pattern on tracing paper. This serves as a test design and can be tinted to check the colors. Using the tracing, mark off borders and hem lines very lightly with pencil on the canvas.

Paint the background, leaving the hems unpainted. For big areas like this, the small cans of latex enamel available in variety and paint stores are more economical than the tiny cans of stencil paint. They are fast-drying and durable too.

Apply the stencil design following the general directions on page 140. Dry thoroughly. Apply two coats of clear plastic varnish. Sand lightly with very fine sandpaper or steel wool, then apply a final coat of varnish.

Turn back the hems on the marked lines, creasing firmly and mitering the corners. Glue the hems in place. If you like, you can glue cotton fringe to the ends.

ANTIQUING FABRICS

Fragments of old fabrics and adaptations of antique prints allow today's needleworkers to almost duplicate the work of old. It is a bonanza needleworkers have never before enjoyed, and we are avidly copying old pieces and designing our own versions of our old favorites. Thread makers, frame manufacturers, and the producers of kits all help feed our desire for reproductions of old needlework.

Sometimes, however, no matter how authentic the reproduction of materials, the finished piece still looks new. Age adds a special kind of softness—yes, and also yellowing and spotting—which just adds to our appreciation of the antique.

While it is really almost impossible to duplicate what the years add to a piece, it is sometimes possible to create the aura of antiquity by treating fabrics with a dye solution made with coffee or tea. It is fun and does add "age" to new products, but be warned: It is not an exact science and what follows does not contain any formulas to be followed to the letter. Don't grab that beautiful cross stitch sampler and run to the kitchen yet!

Anyone who has tried in vain to remove a tea or coffee stain from a good tablecloth can vouch for the fact that these two are fairly permanent and certainly enduring enough to last a long time on a framed piece of needlework or a decorative pillow. Those of us who like the antique look of old laces frequently dye them in coffee or tea solutions and wash the garments by hand with great success. However, this dyeing process should not be used for clothing or other articles that will be washed regularly.

MATERIALS

The materials needed for the dyeing process are all in your kitchen: white vinegar and coffee or tea. Use a ceramic or enamel pot for the dyeing vessel and a long-handled wooden spoon for stirring.

Either coffee or tea may be used for a dye solution. They produce different shades of brown—tea seems to have a more red or orange cast, while coffee is a deeper brown. Both are lovely. The only way to decide which is better for a specific fabric is to make test samples.

Either brewed or instant coffee may be used. Instant is handy when only a small amount is needed. When brewing the coffee or tea for the test sample, record the amounts used. Then to make a larger batch for the actual dye process, the amounts can be increased proportionately.

This color process works only on natural fibers—cotton, linen, silk—and each takes the dye differently. Don't try to antique a fabric which is part synthetic; it is just impossible to get the color to take successfully.

THE DYEING PROCESS

Wash the fabric thoroughly to remove the sizing. If the fabric is one that will ravel, zigzag-stitch the cut ends. Rinse the fabric well and leave it wet, as it must be evenly wet before it is dipped into the dye pot.

Brew the tea or coffee fairly strong, and make enough to fill a pot large enough to allow the fabric to be completely submerged. Bring the brew to a boil in the pot. Add about ½ cup white vinegar per quart of tea or coffee brew. Immerse the wet fabric and boil it about 10 minutes, lifting it out of the dye often to check the depth of coloration. Remember that the fabric will be a little lighter when dry. Rinse well. Roll in a towel, press out excess water, and then iron until dry. Use a small amount of spray starch to restore the sizing if desired.

Immersion is best when a large piece of fabric is to be dyed, but for some projects I prefer to paint the solution on, putting it only on the places I want it. For instance, when antiquing a piece of patchwork, I wet the piece thoroughly, blot it with a towel, then paint the dye on with a camel-hair watercolor brush. I apply the dye heavily on the seam lines, allowing it to bleed into the centers of the pieces. Some of the fabrics in the patchwork may seem to need a heavier application than others, so I work accordingly. While the dye is still wet, I place the patchwork in the clothes dryer and let the heat set the color. Sometimes the heat causes the dye to pull to some spots more heavily than others and really creates an interesting old look.

Actually, the project itself usually dictates the working method I use. For the Doll Quilt I dyed the two printed fabrics before construction by immersing them in the dye solution. Then before quilting I applied more dye along the seam lines and around the edges of the piece. At this time I also painted the antiquing on the seam lines of the muslin squares, leaving the stenciled hearts untouched. The result is a soft old look with interesting shading.

The fabrics for the Country Dolls were all dyed with coffee before construction. Then when the dolls and clothing were finished, more dye was added. To do this I wet the dolls by rubbing water on them just along the seams, and then painted the dye on. Extra color was added to the clothing along the hems and in folds and seams. All were dried in the dryer. The photograph of the doll's face shows the results.

Often the painted-on dye is the most effective. A sampler can be given an antique look by painting the dye solution on the wet linen just around the edges and allowing it to seep into the center portions. A really old-looking sampler is possible if linen and floss are carefully test-dyed before working, then the entire finished piece is dipped and extra color is added in selected places. To test before working, simply tie several short strands of each color floss to the linen, process, and dry. Since cotton floss and linen absorb the dye color differently, some adjustments may have to be made in floss choices.

One word of warning about dyeing already constructed pieces which are stuffed, like the dolls: The dye solution does get into the fiberfill and the odor of coffee is discernible for a few days, but it fades away quickly and is really not a problem.

Now that you know the secrets of giving your projects the treasured family heirloom look, you can start your test samples for that beautiful sampler.

PILLOW CONSTRUCTION

Making up the finished pillow seems to be the most common fear among needleworkers. There are millions of pillow tops tucked away into drawers and work baskets, waiting to be made up. This is silly since the job is really an easy one.

The pillow construction itself takes a short time compared to that needed for most embroidery, and requires basic sewing skills but no extraordinary ability. If you have never made a pillow, it may be a good idea to buy an extra half yard of fabric and make a plain companion pillow before working on the embroidered one. That way you'll gain confidence and expertise—and a complementary pillow.

The materials needed for making a pillow are: appropriate fabric for the back, polyester fiber filling or a pillow form 1″ larger than the pillow dimensions, and matching thread. If you want corded piping in the seam, buy cable cord, a soft white cotton cord found in the drapery department of fabric stores.

Trim the edges of the blocked embroidery ½″ beyond the stitching line. Using this piece as a pattern, cut the backing to the same dimensions.

If corded piping is to be used in the seam, cut a length of cable cord 2″ longer than the total distance around the outside edges of the trimmed embroidery. Cut 1″- to 1¼″-wide bias strips and piece them into a length the same as the cable cord. Fold the bias strip in half lengthwise, insert the cable cord into the fold, and using the zipper foot on your sewing machine, stitch as close to the cord as possible.

With the pillow top right side up, and beginning at the center of the bottom edge, pin the finished piping along the seam line, with its cut edge along the raw edge of the fabric. Clip the cording to the machine stitching at the corners so a sharp right-angle turn can be made. Overlap the ends of the piping and lead them toward the raw edges. Machine-stitch the piping in place, stitching as close to the cord as possible.

Place the backing fabric on a flat surface, right side up. Position the embroidery on top with the wrong side up. Pin the layers together. Sew together on the line of stitching that is holding the piping in place. Leave the bottom partially open to receive the filling. Trim the seams and corners. Turn right side out. Fill with the bulk fiberfill or purchased pillow form. Slip-stitch to close the opening.

Boxed pillows are a little more formal looking than knife-edged ones, but when embroidered or quilted in country designs, they still fit that decorating theme. To make a boxed pillow, follow the previously given steps for making a knife-edged pillow through the point at which the corded piping is sewn to the pillow top. Also make enough piping to reach around the pillow twice and cut four boxing strips 1″ wider than the finished depth and 1″ longer than each of the sides. Seam the four strips in ½″ seams to make a continuous strip. Sew cording to the pillow back in the same way it was sewn to the top. Carefully matching the seam lines to the corners, sew the boxing strip to the pillow top. Next, stitch the free edge of the boxing strip to the pillow backing, again matching the seams to the corners and leaving most of one side open for stuffing. Trim the seams and corners. Turn right side out and insert pillow form or fill with loose fiberfill. Close the opening with small invisible stitches. If you do not use the piping, skip the steps described for the cording.

Ruffled pillows are very appropriate in country interiors and can also be easily constructed. If a double ruffle is to be made, cut the ruffle material twice as wide as the desired finished width plus 1″ for seam allowances. Make the ruffles as full as you like, but not less than double the measurement around the outside edges of the pillow. Piece if necessary, and join the seams of the pieces to make one continuous strip. Fold the strip in half lengthwise, right side out, and pin along the raw edge. With the sewing machine, run two rows of long stitches along the raw edge, placing one on the stitching line ½″ in from the raw edge, the other ⅛″ outside that (or use the gathering foot if preferred). Pull up the gathers to fit the pillow top. Pin the ruffle to the right side of the pillow top, raw edges aligned, allowing extra fullness at the corners so the ruffle will lie flat. Stitch in place with a long stitch setting. Pin the pillow back to the top and finish the pillow following the instructions for using corded piping.

Several pillows in this book have two ruffles trimmed with lace. These are made by simply cutting enough fabric for two single ruffle strips and cutting one ½″ to 1″ wider than the other. Hem one edge of each and sew on lace if desired. Then pin the two ruffles together, right sides up. Gather as for the double ruffle and finish the pillow in the manner described above.

Sometimes the fiberfill seems to show through muslin and country cotton fabrics, giving a bumpy look. You can solve this problem by cutting an extra piece of quilting fleece or batting and using it under the backing fabric. Just baste the two together and treat them as one piece of fabric, or you could quilt them together in a wide diamond pattern on the sewing machine. This does make a pretty and professional-looking pillow.

THE STITCHES

In keeping with the country simplicity of these projects, only the basic and most familiar stitches are used. You can learn these stitches, or refresh your memory, by using these photographs and instructions.

THE STITCHES FOR EMBROIDERY ON FABRIC

BACK STITCH

An easy outline stitch, a row of Back Stitch makes a neat line that bears a close resemblance to machine stitching. The Back Stitch may be worked as an outline or in closely spaced rows to fill space. Worked small, it is an ideal stitch for lettering and curved outlines.

To work: Bring the needle to the surface at point A, which is one stitch length from the beginning of the row, and pull the thread through. Go down at B and come back to the surface at C, keeping the distance from A to B and A to C equal. Pull the thread through to form a stitch. Insert the needle again at A and continue stitching, keeping the stitches as uniform as possible.

BUTTONHOLE STITCH

Sometimes called the Blanket Stitch, Buttonhole can be worked with the loops widely and evenly spaced, as shown in the photograph, or in variations that group the stitches in decorative patterns. When the stitches are placed close together, they become an effective outline with a raised edge.

To work: Bring the needle up at A and pull the thread through. Holding the thread above the needle to form a loop, insert the needle into the fabric at B and bring it back to the surface at C. Pull the needle through, adjusting

Back Stitch

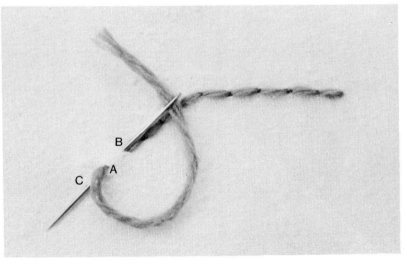

Buttonhole Stitch

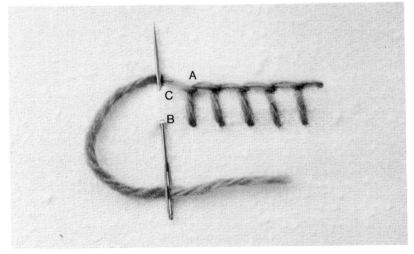

Chain Stitch

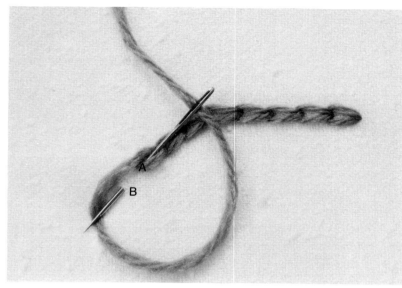

Couching

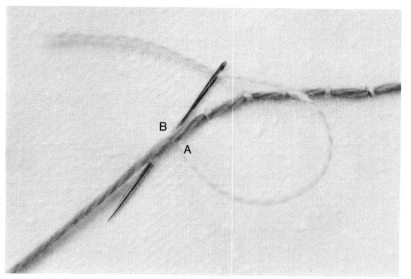

the tension of the loop to allow the stitch to lie flat. Continue in this manner.

CHAIN STITCH

A single row of Chain Stitch forms a broad outline, and closely spaced rows make an effective filling stitch.

To work: Bring the needle up at A, pulling the thread through. Holding the thread below the needle to form a loop, insert the needle again at A, and bring it up at B. Pull the thread through the loop and adjust the tension of the loop. Hold the thread to form another loop, insert the needle at B, and continue.

COUCHING

Couching, actually a method of fastening down long threads on the surface of an embroidery, appears in many variations and fills many needs. It can make a delicate outline or be used for decorative fillings.

To work: Bring the thread to be fastened—the laid thread, shown as the darker thread in the photograph—to the surface at the beginning of the line to be worked, leaving a short tail on the back. Bring the needle, which is threaded with another strand (either the same color or a contrasting one), to the surface at A and insert it again at B on the other side of the laid thread. Pull through, forming a small stitch that fastens the thread in place. These little Couching Stitches may be upright or slightly slanted, as desired. At the end of the line, take the laid thread to the wrong side of the work and cut, leaving a short tail. These short ends need not be fastened or knotted.

TRELLIS COUCHING

Trellis Couching quickly covers a large area with an interesting pattern. The laid and couching threads may be of the same color or of contrasting colors. The Couching Stitch may be the simple upright form shown in the photograph, or may be another ornamental stitch. The diamond-shaped openings can be left open as shown, or may be decorated with a small detached stitch.

To work: Stitch the long straight stitches in diagonal parallel lines, filling the shape of the motif. Bring the needle, threaded with the couching thread, to the surface at *A* and pull the thread through. Make the tie-down stitch by inserting the needle at *B* and bringing it up again at *C*, in position for the beginning of the next stitch. Fasten each intersection of the laid threads in this way.

CROSS STITCH

Equally at home on canvas or fabric, the Cross Stitch is very easy, but beautiful and effective. The secret of perfect Cross Stitch is to have all the base stitches slanting in one direction throughout the work.

When making multiple stitches in one color, it is best to work across making the base stitches (shown by the slanted stitch *A* to *B* in the photograph) and then return, placing the second stitches on top as shown. Complete single stitches individually.

To work: Bring the needle to the surface at *A* and pull the thread through. Insert the needle at *B* and bring it up again at *C*, which is directly below *B* and on a line to the right of *A*. Pull the thread through to form the slanted stitch. Continue to the end of the row. Return by working as shown, inserting the needle and bringing it to the surface in the holes made by the previous stitches.

Cross Stitch can be worked on a closely woven fabric, as in the photograph, or on even-weave fabric which has an open weave with individual

Trellis Couching

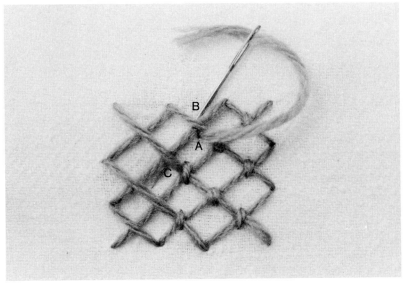

Cross Stitch

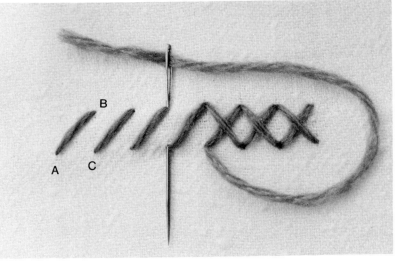

threads apparent, or on needlepoint canvas—all in exactly the same way. When using needlepoint canvas or a fabric where the threads can be counted, determine the number of threads the Cross Stitch will cover and be sure to cover the same number with each stitch.

FISHBONE STITCH

The Fishbone Stitch is an ideal filling for many floral and leaf shapes and thus is a very useful embroidery stitch.

To work: Bring the needle up at A, pull the thread through, and go down at B, which is about ¼″ down the center line from A. (The first stitch should be made fairly long to ensure that the side stitches lie on a good slant.) Come up at C, which is to the left and very slightly below A on the outline. Holding the thread below the needle to form a loop, go down at D, which corresponds to C but is to the right of A. Bring the needle to the surface again at B and pull the thread through, adjusting the loop so the stitch lies flat (end of step 1 in photograph).

Make a small stitch across the loop by inserting the needle at E as shown in step 2. Come up at F on the left side and repeat the loop-forming and tie-down stitches until the area is covered. Adjust the lengths of the stitches along the outline as needed to retain the shape of the motif.

FRENCH KNOT

This interesting little knot serves many purposes—indeed, it would be hard to imagine embroidery without the charm of French Knots. They can be used singly as in seeding, packed together to form solid textured areas, or worked in rows as an outline.

To work: Bring the needle to the surface at A and pull the thread

Fishbone Stitch

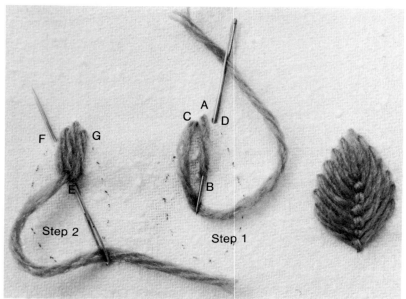

French Knot

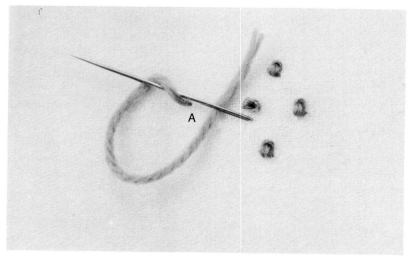

through. Wrap the thread around the needle once; then insert the tip of the needle into the fabric close to *A* but with at least one thread of fabric intervening. Pull the thread to tighten it snugly around the needle. Pull the needle through to the back of the work.

FRENCH KNOT ON A LONG THREAD

This is a useful variation of the French Knot that can be worked to form flower centers, miniature trees, and leaves.

To work: Bring the needle to the surface at *A* and pull the thread through. Wrap the thread around the needle once. Insert the tip of the needle into the fabric at *B* and pull the thread to tighten the wrap around the needle. Pull the needle through to the back of the work.

OUTLINE STITCH

As its name suggests, this stitch forms a neat outline and as such it is one of the workhorses of embroidery. When working, the thread should always be thrown in the same direction—either above or below the needle.

To work: Bring the needle to the surface at *A* and pull the thread through. With the thread above (or below) the needle, go down at *B* and come up at *C*, exactly halfway between *A* and *B*. Pull the thread through and continue stitching.

RUNNING STITCH

This basic hand-sewing stitch, good also for embroidery, happens also to be the stitch used for quilting.

Work as shown in the photograph, keeping the stitches on top slightly longer than those on the back. Try to maintain an even stitch length.

French Knot on a Long Thread

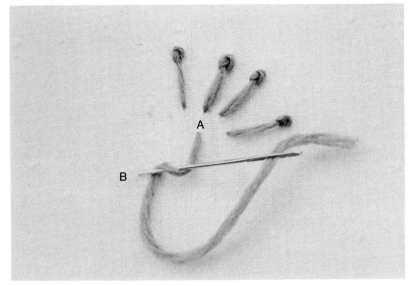

Outline Stitch

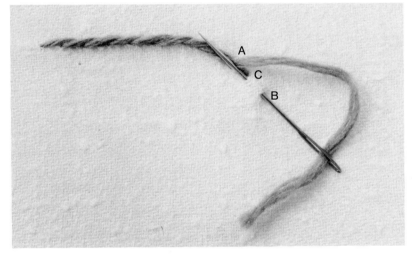

Running Stitch

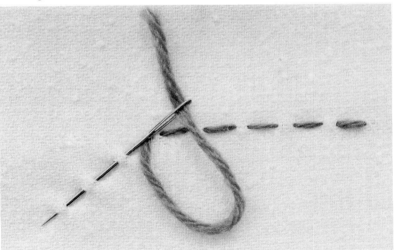

Whipped Running Stitch

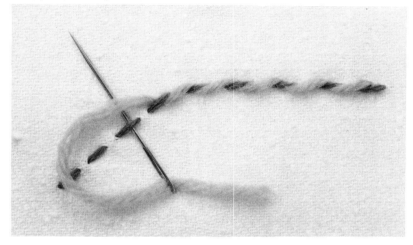

Satin Stitch

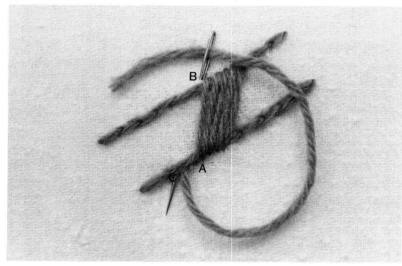

Seeding

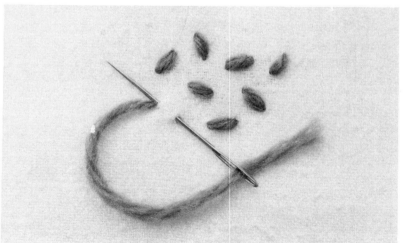

WHIPPED RUNNING STITCH

This is a very quick decorative two-color line stitch. First work a row of Running Stitch. With another color thread, bring the needle up just under the center of the first Running Stitch. Without piercing the fabric, slide the needle upward under the second Running Stitch. Continue along the row, always inserting the needle upward with the thread in the position shown.

SATIN STITCH

One of the loveliest of embroidery stitches, Satin is aptly named, for when properly worked it has a smooth, lustrous look. A Split Stitch outline underneath adds depth and eases the task of making an even outside edge. Extra padding in the form of long stitches can be added between the outline stitches before the Satin Stitch is applied.

To work as photographed: Outline the area with small Split Stitches in the color that will be used for the Satin Stitch. Begin the Satin Stitch by bringing the needle to the surface at *A* and pulling the thread through. Make a slanting stitch by taking the needle down at *B* and bringing it up again at *C*, which is close to *A*. Pull the thread through and continue stitching in this manner until the area is covered.

SEEDING

Seeding is ideal as a light filling for flowers, leaves, and even backgrounds where just a slight texture and a little color are needed.

To work: Make tiny straight stitches and place them at random. The ones shown in the photograph are made double—two stitches in each place. This makes them nice and plump and a little raised. Single stitches can be used where a lighter texture is needed.

SPLIT STITCH

Hardworking little Split Stitch, which looks like a scaled-down version of Chain Stitch, does many embroidery jobs. It is a lovely fine outlining stitch, is often used as a padding under other stitches, and can be worked in closely spaced rows as a solid filling.

To work: Bring the needle up at *A* and pull the yarn through. Go down at *B* and come up at *C*, keeping the space between *A* and *C* equal to that between *A* and *B*. Pull the yarn through, forming a small flat stitch between *A* and *B*. Insert the needle down into the center of the stitch just formed, splitting it as shown in the photograph. Continue across the row.

STRAIGHT STITCH

The Straight Stitch is an uncomplicated flat stitch often used as an accent or scattered to add texture to a large otherwise plain area. The slant and length of the stitches can vary to suit the need.

To work: Simply place the stitches at the desired angle, following the stitching order from *A* to *B* to *C*.

THE STITCHES FOR EMBROIDERY ON CANVAS

BASKET WEAVE STITCH

The Basket Weave Stitch does not cause great stretching of the canvas and is therefore the favored plain needlepoint stitch for filling. It is a bit tricky to work in the beginning, but is not nearly as difficult as it is believed to be. Try it first within the confines of a square shape, until you master the stitching pattern; then try an irregular shape. Many times it is helpful to outline the irregular shape with the Continental Stitch and then work the Basket Weave within the outline.

To work: Begin at the upper right

Split Stitch

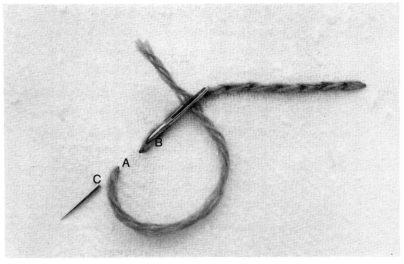

Straight Stitch

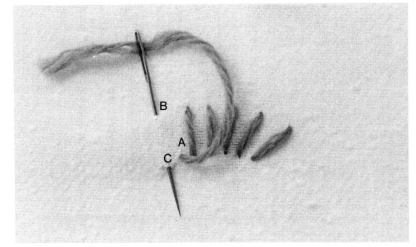

Basket Weave Stitch

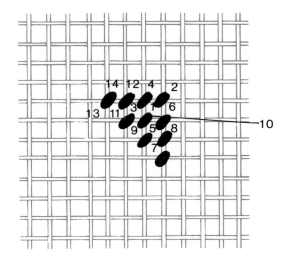

Continental Stitch

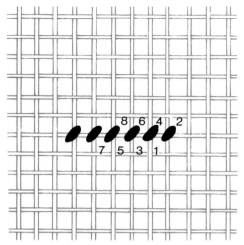

Upright Gobelin Stitch

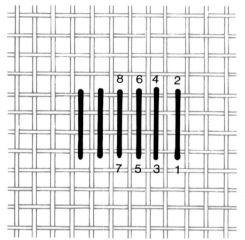

Bargello Stitch

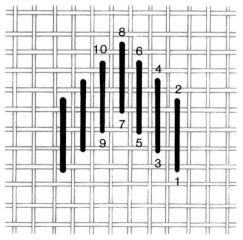

corner with the first stitch and work following the numbers in the diagram. Note that after a few rows have been worked, there is a definite woven pattern on the back: the rows are diagonal and alternating—one row worked upward followed by one row in the downward direction, and so on. Keep this sequence or a ridge that can't be blocked out will develop!

CONTINENTAL STITCH

The Continental Stitch is worked in rows across the canvas beginning at the top right side. The row is worked in the numbered sequence shown on the diagram. When the end of the row is reached, the canvas is turned and the return row worked.

UPRIGHT GOBELIN STITCH

Bargello is based on the Upright Gobelin Stitch, using variations in how it is placed on the canvas. When worked across the canvas in rows as diagrammed, the Upright Gobelin creates a strong horizontal line. The stitch length can vary according to need; stitches sewn over two to six threads are the most practical.

To work: Follow the numbers on the chart, taking care to smooth each stitch so it lies flat on the canvas.

BARGELLO STITCH

Bargello designs are created when Upright Gobelin Stitches are placed so they move up or down the canvas in a pattern.

Work the stitches as you do the Upright Gobelin, following a Bargello chart for placement.

INDEX